LAST DAYS FABLES

A rebuttal of *Last Days Madness* by
Preterist Gary DeMar

Gerald B. Shugart

Lulu Publishing | Morrisville, North Carolina

Last Days
Fables

by

Gerald B. Shugart

Formatting conducted by ShelfBloom ePress. Concerns about formatting, typographical errors, etc. should be sent to support@shelfbloom.com

DEDICATION

This book is dedicated to J. Michael Schroeder, from whom I first heard the glorious gospel of the grace of God, the gospel of my salvation.

"How beautiful upon the mountains are the feet of him that bringeth good tidings, that publisheth peace; that bringeth good tidings of good, that publisheth salvation" (Isa.52:7).

Table of Contents

Chapter I | Introduction   1
Chapter II | The End of the Age   4
Chapter III | Things Coming on the World   10
Chapter IV | The Coming of the Son of Man   16
Chapter V | Is Israel's Land Prophetically Significant?   20
Chapter VI | The Kingdom Age   26
Chapter VII | The Kingdom Age; Part 2   34
Chapter VIII | Will the Kingdom be Restored to Israel?   41
Chapter IX | The Return of the Lord Jesus to the Earth   48
Chapter X | Timing Is Everything   54
Chapter XI | Daniel's Seventy Weeks   65
Chapter XII | Daniel's Seventy Weeks; Part 2   73
Chapter XIII | This Generation   79
Chapter XIV | "Shall Not Taste Death" -- Matthew   86
16:27-28
Chapter XV | You Will Not Finish Going Through the   93
Towns of Israel
Chapter XVI | The Destruction of the Temple in the   98
First Century
Chapter XVII | Gospel of the Kingdom Preached in the   103
Whole World?
Chapter XVIII |The Olive Tree   110
Chapter XIX | God Hath Not Cast Away His People   114
Chapter XX | Conclusion   121

Chapter I. Introduction

Preterism is a system of interpreting the Scriptures which relates to "eschatology," which is defined as the part of theology concerned with the final events of history or a study of the Last Days. The "preter" in "preter-ism" comes from the Latin word "praeter," and one of the meanings of that word is "past."[1] So in essence a Preterist can be described as a theologian who asserts that almost all of the prophecies found in the Bible have already been fulfilled and therefore belong to "past" history.

Gary DeMar writes that *"New Testament preterism relates to prophecies that were fulfilled in events leading up to and including the destruction of the temple and the judgment on the city of Jerusalem that took place in A.D. 70,* **in particular, the Olivet Discourse in the Synoptic Gospels (Matt. 24; Mark 13; Luke 21)**, *the Man of Lawlessness (2 Thess. 2), passages related to the Antichrist (1 John 2:18, 22; 4:3; 2 John 7), and, of course, Revelation (1:1, 3; 22:10)"* [*emphasis added*]. [2]

DeMar also writes that *"Beyond A.D.70, Israel as a nation plays no prophetic role."* [3]

I am using the writings of Gary DeMar to expose the errors of what is called "Partial Preterism" as it is being taught today. I do not want any of my following remarks to be construed as impunging his sincerity or character. However, his lack of knowledge about the Last Days results in one blunder after another and it is a simple task to prove that his theology is bankrupt.

For instance, in regard to the Olivet Discourse he wrote that *"The generation to whom Jesus was speaking would not pass away until all those things listed in Matthew 24:1-34 came to pass."* [4]

DeMar's mistaken ideas are based largely on the Olivet discourse and his interpretation of the Lord Jesus' answer to His disciple's following question: " *'Tell us,' they said, 'when will this happen, and what will be the sign of your coming and **of the end of the age?** '"* (Mt. 24:3; NIV). [5]

In regard to this verse DeMar correctly writes: *"Notice the disciples did not ask about the end of the 'world' (kosmos), as some Bible versions translate the Greek word 'aion'...**they asked about the end of the 'age'"*** [emphasis added]. [6]

We will now see that earlier in the gospel of Matthew the Lord Jesus spoke about the events which will happen at the end of the age and it is certain that those events did not take place in A.D. 70, as Gary DeMar asserts.

End Notes

1. Adam Alexander, *A Compendious Dictionary of the Latin Tongue* [Edinburgh, Scotland: C. Stewart, 1814], 550.

2. Gary DeMar, "Is Gary DeMar Secretly a Friend to Hyperpreterists?" *The American Vision*; Accessed December 27, 2018, https://americanvision.org/3032/is-gary-demar-secretly-a-friend-to-hyperpreterists/

3. Gary DeMar, *Last Days Madness* (American Vision, 1999, Fourth Revised Edition), 398.

4. *Ibid.*, 15.

5. All Scripture quotations, unless otherwise indicated, are taken from the. Holy Bible, New International Version (NIV).

6. Gary DeMar, *Last Days Madness*, 69.

Chapter II. The End of the Age

In the following passage the Lord Jesus spoke the parable of the "tares of the field" where He described what will happen at the "end of the age":

"Then he left the crowd and went into the house. His disciples came to him and said, 'Explain to us the parable of the weeds in the field.' He answered, 'The one who sowed the good seed is the Son of Man. **The field is the world (kosmos)**, *and the good seed stands for the people of the kingdom. The weeds are the people of the evil one, and the enemy who sows them is the devil.* **The harvest is the end of the age (aion)**, *and the harvesters are angels.* **'As the weeds are pulled up and burned in the fire, so it will be at the end of the age (aion).** *The Son of Man will send out his angels, and they will weed out of his kingdom everything that causes sin and all who do evil. They will throw them into the blazing furnace, where there will be weeping and gnashing of teeth. Then the righteous will shine like the sun in the kingdom of their Father"* (Mt. 13:36-43).

Here we can see that the Lord Jesus speaks of a harvest that will happen at the "end of the age." He also makes it clear that the harvest will take place in the field, and He says that the "field is the world (*kosmos*)."

Kosmos

The Greek word translated "world" is *kosmos* and it means *"the inhabitants of the earth, men, the human race...Mt. xiii. 38."* [1]

In his remarks on verse 38 where the Lord Jesus used the

Greek word *kosmos* Gary DeMar says the following:

*"Verse 38 is correct to say 'world,' for the Greek word is ' kosmos'--**a common Greek word translated 'world.' It refers to the entire system of this planet and the order of things**"* [*emphasis added*]. [2]

At another place DeMar affirms the meaning of the word *kosmos* which he gave there by saying that the word refers to the whole world: *"Earlier in his letter to the Colossians, Paul describes how the gospel was 'constantly bearing fruit and increasing **in all the world [kosmos]**' (1:6). The faith of the Romans was 'being proclaimed throughout **the whole world [kosmos]' (Rom. 1: 8), 'to all nations' (16:26)**"* [*emphasis added*]. [3]

Gary DeMar's understanding of the meaning of the word *"kosmos"* is the same meaning that those living in the first century would have put on that word. So the Jews who heard the Lord's words at Matthew 13:38 they would have understood that when the Lord Jesus spoke of the "field" to be harvested being the *kosmos* they would have also understood that at the *"end of the age"* that a harvest would come upon the whole world--upon all nations

The End of the Age

In an article titled "Wheat, Tares and the Kingdom" Gary DeMar correctly understands that at Matthew 13:36-43 the Lord was speaking about what will happen at the "end of the age":

*"The thing coming to an end in this teaching is not the world itself, but a particular long period of time. Jesus is not concerned with the end of the world, **but the end of the age. The judgment that is described here, therefore, pertains to the end of that period of time**"* [*emphasis added*]. [4]

Therefore, the Lord Jesus' answer to His disciple's

following question was not just about the destruction of Jerusalem in A.D. 70 but instead an answer about a harvest which will come upon the whole earth at the "end of the age':

"'Tell us,' they said, 'when will this happen, and what will be the sign of your coming and of **the end of the age?**'" (Mt. 24:3).

Gather Out of the Kingdom

Here we see that the 'tares' will be gathered out of the kingdom:

"As therefore **the tares are gathered and burned in the fire**; so shall it be in the end of this age. The Son of man shall send forth his angels, and **they shall gather out of his kingdom all things that offend, and them which do iniquity; And shall cast them into a furnace of fire**: there shall be wailing and gnashing of teeth. Then shall the righteous shine forth as the sun in the kingdom of their Father" (Mt. 13:41-43).

It is evident that all things which offend were not gathered out of the world (kosmos) and a harvest did not come unto all nations in the first century so the events in regard to the "end of the age" remain in the future. Despite these facts Gary DeMar wrote the following:

"Matthew 13:24-30, 36-43 describe the judgment that would come upon **unbelieving Jerusalem**. During this time, the angels would 'gather out of his kingdom all things that offend, and them which do iniquity' (13:41) and these would be judged with fire" [emphasis added]. [5]

So despite the fact that the Lord Jesus spoke of a harvest where the field to be harvested is the kosmos and Gary DeMar understands that the kosmos includes "all nations" he now asserts that the harvest was limited to unbelieving Jerusalem!

Gary DeMar has a distorted view concerning just what the words "end of the age" mean because he says that "*the destruction of the temple inaugurates a new era in which 'the blood of Christ' cleanses our 'conscience from dead works to serve the living God' (Heb.9:14). Therefore, the expression 'end of the age' refers to the end of ' the Jewish age.' i.e.,* **the time of transference from a national [Israel only] to an international people of God [the world]**" *[emphasis added].* [6]

Evidently DeMar is unaware of the fact that Paul was preaching gospel truths to the international people of God many years before the destruction of the temple in AD 70. In fact, when Paul wrote his epistle to the church at Colosse he was being held captive in Rome (Col. 4:10) and by then he said that the gospel had gone out to "the whole world":

"*...you have already heard in the true message of the gospel that has come to you. In the same way,* **the gospel is bearing fruit and growing throughout the whole world**--*just as it has been doing among you since the day you heard it and truly understood God's grace*" (Col. 1:5-6).

The facts presented from the Scriptures demonstrate in no uncertain terms that at the end of the age there will be a world-wide harvest when all the unbelievers will be taken out of the world. Despite these facts Gary Demar insists that at the end of the age has already happened and the harvest only came upon Jerusalem. In fact, his whole teaching about the End of the Age is totally dependent on the idea that the harvest which will happen at the end of the age does not involve the whole world. Then he says:

"*Unfortunately, the clear testimony of the Bible does not convince those who are intent on making the Bible fit their preconceived view of prophecy.*" [7]

We can see that the clear testimony of the Bible does not convince Gary DeMar that his preconceived view of prophecy is in error.

He continues teaching his "myth" that the "end of the age" has already happened in the past and in doing so he must turn "away his ears from the truth." The first thing that the Lord Jesus said when answering His Apostle's question concerning what will happen at the "end of the age" was:

"Watch out that no one deceives you" (Mt. 24:4).

Gary DeMar is unwittingly deceiving others about the teaching of the Scriptures concerning the Last Days and the following passage describes him perfectly:

"For the time will come when they will not endure sound doctrine; but after their own lusts shall they heap to themselves teachers, having itching ears; And they shall turn away their ears from the truth, and shall be turned unto fables" (2 Tim. 4:3-4; KJV).

End Notes

1. Joseph Henry Thayer, *A Greek-English Lexicon of the New Testament* (Grand Rapids: Baker Books, 1977), 357.

2. Gary DeMar, "Wheat, Tares and the Kingdom," *American Vision*; Accessed December 15,2018, https://americanvision.org/3962/wheat-tares-mustard-leaven/

3. Gary DeMar, *Last Days Madness*, 87-88.

4. Gary DeMar, "Wheat, Tares and the Kingdom," *American Vision*.

5. *Ibid.*

6. Gary DeMar, *Last Days Madness*, 70.

7. *Ibid.*, 402.

Chapter III. Things Coming on the World

The "great tribulation" spoken of by the Lord Jesus in the following passage will be strictly in regard to Israel and after it is over signs will appear in the sky:

*"For then shall be **great tribulation**, such as was not since the beginning of the world to this time, no, nor ever shall be. And except those days should be shortened, there should no flesh be saved: but for the elect's sake those days shall be shortened....**Immediately after the tribulation of those days shall the sun be darkened, and the moon shall not give her light**, and the stars shall fall from heaven, and the powers of the heavens shall be shaken"* (Mt. 24:21-22,29; KJV).

Then after the signs will be seen in the sky there will be fear among nations while anticipating the things which will be coming upon the world:

*"**There will be signs in the sun, moon and stars.** On the earth, nations will be in anguish and perplexity at the roaring and tossing of the sea. **People will faint from terror, apprehensive of what is coming on the world (oikoumene)**, for the heavenly bodies will be shaken. At that time they will see the Son of Man coming in a cloud with power and great glory"* (Lk. 21:25-27).

The first thing that must be understood about the events described here is the fact that the great tribulation will be over by the time when the signs are seen in the sky. So the events described at Luke 21:25-27 have nothing to do with the great tribulation and therefore are events which will occur upon the rest of the world (*oikoumene*).

Oikoumene

At Luke 21: 26 we can can see that there will be distress of nations on the earth because the people of the nations will *"faint from terror, apprehensive of what is coming on the world (**oikoumene**)."*

According to Joseph Henry Thayer the Greek word *oikoumene* in this instance means *"the whole inhabited earth, the world...Lk.iv. 5; xxi. 26"* [1]

Gary DeMar gives the meaning for the word "oikoumene" here:

*"The case can be made that 'oikoumene' is used exclusively for the geographical area generally limited to the Roman empire of the first-century and the territories immediately adjacent which were known and accessible to first-century travelers. **When first-century Christians read the word 'oikoumene,' they thought of what they knew of their world**" [emphasis mine].* [2]

Therefore, we can know that after the great tribulation is over that there will be things coming on the earth which will terrorize people over an area of the earth much greater that just Jerusalem and Judea:

*"**People will faint from terror, apprehensive of what is coming on the world**, for the heavenly bodies will be shaken"* (Lk. 21:26).

On the Face of the Whole Earth

Later in the same discourse found in the book of Luke we see even more evidence that the events under discussion will be world wide and not just limited to the surroundings of Judea:

"Be careful, or your hearts will be weighed down with

11

carousing, drunkenness and the anxieties of life, and that day will close on you suddenly like a trap. **For it will come on all those who live on the face of the whole earth**" (Lk. 21:34-35).

Here the word "earth" is translated from the Greek word *ge* and in this instance it means "*'the inhabited earth,' the abode of men and animals: Lk. xxi.35.*" [3]

The context demands this meaning of the word because just eight verses previously the Lord Jesus spoke of things coming upon the world. The Preterists say that the word *ge* as it is used in this verse means Israel and that is one of its meanings if the context indicates it is referring to Israel. However, Joseph Henry Thayer says the following about the meaning the Preterists put on the word:

"*'a country, land, enclosed within fixed boundries, a tract of land, territory, region';* **simply, when it is plain from the context what land is meant, as that of the Jews: Lk. iv. 25; xxi. 23; Ro. ix.28; Jas. v. 17**" [*emphasis added*]. **4**

There is absolutely nothing in the immediate context that even hints that the word refers to Israel but on the other hand the context does indicate that the Greek word in view is described as the inhabited world.

Revelation 6:12-16 and 14:14-16

In a parallel passage to Luke 21:25-27 we can see that after the signs in the heavens "nations" will indeed be in distress:

"...**The sun turned black like sackcloth made of goat hair, the whole moon turned blood red and the stars in the sky fell to earth**...Then **the kings of the earth, the princes, the generals, the rich, the mighty, and everyone else, both slave and free**, *hid in caves and among the rocks of the mountains. They called to the mountains and the rocks, 'Fall* *on us and hide us from the face of him who sits on the throne and from the wrath of the Lamb!'"* (Rev. 6:12-16).

Here the Apostle John describes the things which will occur after the signs in the sky, and it is clear that these events are not limited to the land of Judea: *"the kings of the earth"* and *"everyone else, both slave and free"*. Despite this Gary DeMar denies that these verses are speaking of a world wide judgment and says that they are only speaking about the destruction of Jerusalem in A.D.70:

*"**As Jerusalem's destruction drew near for that generation**, 'they said to the mountains and the rocks, Fall on us and hide us from the presence of Him who sits on the throne, and from the wrath of the Lamb; for the great day of their wrath has come; and who is able to stand?' (Rev. 6:16-17)"* [emphasis mine].[5]

Later in the book of Revelation we can see a parallel passage of the world-wide harvest of which the Lord Jesus spoke at Matthew 13:37-43 which will happen at the end of the age:

*"I looked, and there before me was a white cloud, and seated on the cloud was one like a son of man with a crown of gold on his head and a sharp sickle in his hand. Then another angel came out of the temple and called in a loud voice to him who was sitting on the cloud, 'Take your sickle and reap, because the time to reap has come, **for the harvest of the earth is ripe.**' So he who was seated on the cloud swung his sickle over the earth, and **the earth was harvested**"* (Rev. 14:14-16).

The facts revealed in the twenty first chapter of the gospel of Luke reveal that in the Olivet Discourse the Lord Jesus was speaking about a world wide harvest and despite these facts Gary DeMar insists that the events described in this chapter happened in the past:

*"**New Testament preterism relates to prophecies that were fulfilled in events leading up to and including the destruction of the temple and the judgment on the city of**"*

Jerusalem that took place in A.D. 70, in particular, the Olivet Discourse in the Synoptic Gospels (Matt. 24; Mark 13; **Luke 21**), the Man of Lawlessness (2 Thess. 2), passages related to the Antichrist (1 John 2:18, 22; 4:3; 2 John 7), and, of course, Revelation (1:1, 3; 22:10)" [emphasis added][6]

End Notes

1. Joseph Henry Thayer, *A Greek English Lexicon of the New Testament*, 441.

2. Gary DeMar, *The Gospel Preached to All the World*, Part 3 of 4; Accessed November 22, 2018, https://www.preteristarchive.com/Modern/2003_demar_all-the-world.html

3. Joseph Henry Thayer, *A Greek-English Lexicon of the New Testament*, 114.

4. *Ibid.*, 115.

5. Gary DeMar, *Last Days Madness*, 125.

6. Gary DeMar, "Is Gary DeMar Secretly a Friend to Hyperpreterists?" *The American Vision*; Accessed December 27, 2018, https://americanvision.org/3032/is-gary-demar-secretly-a-friend-to-hyperpreterists/

Chapter IV. The Coming of the Son of Man

Here we see that when the Lord Jesus returns to the earth there will be a world wide judgment:

*"Enoch, the seventh from Adam, prophesied about them: 'See, **the Lord is coming** with thousands upon thousands of his holy ones **to judge everyone**, and to convict all of them of all the ungodly acts they have committed in their ungodliness, and of all the defiant words ungodly sinners have spoken against him'"* (Jude 14-15).

That prophecy is referring to the same thing found in the following passage, where the Lord Jesus is seen taking vengeance on everyone who does not know God:

*"God is just: He will pay back trouble to those who trouble you and give relief to you who are troubled, and to us as well. This will happen when **the Lord Jesus is revealed from heaven** in blazing fire with his powerful angels. **He will punish those who do not know God and do not obey the gospel of our Lord Jesus**"* (2 Thess. 1:6-8).

All Nations Will Be Judged

Indeed, we can see that those from "all nations" will be judged when the Lord Jesus returns to the earth:

*"When the Son of Man comes in his glory, and all the angels with him, he will sit on his glorious throne. **All the nations will be gathered before him**, and he will separate the people one from another as a shepherd separates the sheep from the goats. He will put the sheep on his right and the*

goats on his left...Then he will say to those on his left,
**'*Depart from me, you who are cursed, into the eternal fire*
prepared for the devil and his angels.'**" (Mt. 25:31-33, 41).

Now let us look at the following verse and then see Gary DeMar's interpretation of it:

"*Then will appear the sign of the Son of Man in heaven.*
**And then all the peoples of the earth will mourn when they
see the Son of Man coming on the clouds of heaven, with
power and great glory**" (Mt. 24:30).

Gary DeMar writes: "*The 'coming' of 'the Son of Man' is
most often taught as a worldwide event since Jesus states
that 'all the tribes of the earth will mourn' (Matt.24:30).
Again, most Bible translations do not capture the true
meaning of the Greek. A better translation is 'tribes of the
land,' indicating that **the event is restricted to Israel** since
Israel is the topic of discussion*" [*emphasis mine*]. [1]

It is clear that the coming of the Lord Jesus mentioned at
Matthew 24:30 is a world wide event and that fact alone
sinks the ship of the teaching called Preterism. In A.D.70
there was no world wide judgment so a person must throw
reason to the wind in order to think that the coming of the
Lord Jesus mentioned in the 24th chapter of Matthew was
fulfilled in A.D.70!

The Great Flood

Matthew uses the example of the great flood to illustrate
the fact that when the Lord Jesus returns to the earth it will
be a worldwide judgment:

"**As it was in the days of Noah, so it will be at the
coming of the Son of Man.** *For in the days before the flood,
people were eating and drinking, marrying and giving in
marriage, up to the day Noah entered the ark;* **and they knew
nothing about what would happen until the flood came and**

took them all away. That is how it will be at the coming of the Son of Man" (Mt. 24:37-39).

When we examine the events which will happen during the "second woe" it is certain that this prophecy was not fulfilled in A.D. 70:

*"The first woe is past; two other woes are yet to come. The sixth angel sounded his trumpet, and I heard a voice coming from the four horns of the golden altar that is before God. It said to the sixth angel who had the trumpet, 'Release the four angels who are bound at the great river Euphrates.' And the four angels who had been kept ready for this very hour and day and month and year **were released to kill a third of mankind**"* (Rev. 9:12-15).

Perhaps Gary DeMar will tell us when a third of mankind were killed by A.D. 70 since he says that the events described in the book of Revelation were fulfilled during the lifetimes of those who originally received that book:

"As a preterist, I will defend the view that Revelation is about events that were to happen soon for those living in John's day, in particular, in events leading up to and including the end of the Old Covenant represented outwardly by the temple and Israel's center of worship, Jerusalem." [2]

End Notes

1. Gary DeMar, *Last Days Madness*, 166.

2. Gary DeMar, "Reading Revelation with Biblical Eyes," *The American Vision*; Accessed February 3, 2019, https://americanvision.org/7052/reading-revelation-with-biblical-eyes/

Chapter V. Is Israel's Land Prophetically Significant?

In an article tiltled *Is Israel's Land Prophetically Significant?* Gary DeMar quotes the following passage from the book of Joshua:

"So the LORD gave Israel all the land which He had sworn to give to their fathers, and they possessed it and lived in it. And the LORD gave them rest on every side, according to all that He had sworn to their fathers, and no one of all their enemies stood before them; the LORD gave all their enemies into their hand. Not one of the good promises which the LORD had made to the house of Israel failed; all came to pass (Joshua 21:43-45).

DeMar then makes the following comments on this passage:

"All the elements necessary for the fulfillment of the Abrahamic covenant as related to the land are present in these verses: God gave the Israelites the land He had promised to give; they possessed and lived in the land; they had rest; their enemies did not stand before them; not one of the promises God made to the house of Israel failed. If these verses do not teach what they seem to teach, then how else could God have put it, said it, or written it if He had wanted to inform the Israelites that they had in fact possessed the land as promised? Even after being confronted with these crystal clear words from Joshua, futurists continue to insist that they do not teach what they say. [1]

DeMar is in error when he asserts that futurists insist that the words of Joshua do not teach what they say but instead he is ignorant of the following prophecies concerning the land which were revealed after the book of Joshua was written.

These prophecies represent an integral part the promises which were made by the LORD in regard to Israel and the land:

"*My eyes will watch over them for their good, and **I will bring them back to this land**. I will build them up and not tear them down; **I will plant them and not uproot them**"* (Jer. 24:6).

The LORD promises that He will bring the Israelites back to the land and will not uproot them. We see the same promises repeated by the prophet Amos:

"*I will bring my people Israel back from exile. 'They will rebuild the ruined cities and live in them. They will plant vineyards and drink their wine; they will make gardens and eat their fruit. **I will plant Israel in their own land, never again to be uprooted from the land I have given them,**' says the LORD your God*" (Amos 9:14-15).

These prophecies were certainly not fulfilled at any time in the first century because as late as the second Jewish revolt (A. D. 132-135) the Jews were excluded from Jerusalem upon penalty of death.

Now let us look at the "land" promises of the LORD under the Davidic covenant:

"*Now therefore so shalt thou say unto my servant David...I will appoint a place for my people Israel, **and will plant them, that they may dwell in a place of their own, and move no more; neither shall the children of wickedness afflict them any more**, as beforetime*" (2 Sam. 7:8,10; KJV).

There has never been a time when the children of Israel were brought back to the land which the LORD gave to Jacob and were moved no more, unless that prophecy is being fulfilled right now. And there has never been a time when they were brought back to the land and were moved no more and the Israelites were not afflicted by their enemies because at this time they are being afflicted by their enemies. Therefore, we can understand that in the future these prophecies concerning Israel and the land will be fulfilled. After all, the LORD said that He would not alter the promises He made to David and He also said that He will not lie to David:

*"I have made a covenant with my chosen one, I have sworn to David my servant...I will not take my love from him, nor will I ever betray my faithfulness. **I will not violate my covenant or alter what my lips have uttered.** Once for all, I have sworn by my holiness-- **and I will not lie to David**"* (Ps. 89:3,33-35).

The following prophecy speaks of the time when the promise the LORD made to David concerning the land and the Israelites living in peace will be fulfilled:

*"They will live **in the land I gave to my servant Jacob, the land where your ancestors lived. They and their children and their children's children will live there forever**, and David my servant will be their prince forever. I will make a covenant of peace with them; it will be an everlasting covenant. I will establish them and increase their numbers, and **I will put my sanctuary among them forever.** My dwelling place will be with them; I will be their God, and they will be my people. Then the nations will know that I the LORD make Israel holy, when my sanctuary is among them forever "* (Ezek. 37:25-28).

By the time this prophecy will be fulfilled the prophecy concerning the New Covenant which Paul refers to in the following verse will also be fulfilled:

*"And so **all Israel shall be saved**: as it is written, There shall come out of Sion the Deliverer, and shall turn away ungodliness from Jacob: **For this is my covenant unto them, when I shall take away their sins**"* (Ro. 11:26-27).

Gary DeMar writes the following about this verse:

"But the question that arises from modern Zionists, dispensationalists, and others who wish to see some form of restored physical Israel and temple, is whether God intends

22

to save the whole physical nation of Israelites in the future. **Does Paul's argument that 'all Israel will be saved' pertain to physical, ethnic Israel? I think the context makes that impossible**" [*emphasis added*]. [2]

When we look at the following passage from the Old Testament which speaks of the new Covenant promised to Israel we will see that DeMar is in error:

"*Behold, the days come, saith the LORD, that I will make a **new covenant** with the house of Israel, and with the house of Judah: **Not according to the covenant that I made with their fathers in the day that I took them by the hand to bring them out of the land of Egypt; which my covenant they brake**, although I was an husband unto them, saith the LORD: But this shall be the covenant that I will make with the house of Israel; After those days, saith the LORD, I will put my law in their inward parts, and write it in their hearts; and will be their God, and they shall be my people. And they shall teach no more every man his neighbour, and every man his brother, saying, Know the LORD: **for they shall all know me, from the least of them unto the greatest of them, saith the LORD: for I will forgive their iniquity, and I will remember their sin no more**"* (Jer. 31:31-34).

The LORD says that He will make a New Covenant with the house of Israel and the house of Judah. The "fathers" of those who will partake of this covenant were the children of Israel who the LORD redeemed out of Egypt and the same people who broke His covenant (Jer.11:1-8). Since the "fathers" of these future members of the houses of Israel and Judah were the physical descendants of Abraham, Isaac and Jacob then that can only mean that in the future the members of both houses will also be the physical descendants of Abraham, Isaac and Jacob. So in the future there will be a generation made up of the physical descendants of Jacob (Israel) who will all know the LORD and all of them will have their sins forgiven and be saved. Since that has never happened in the past that explains why Paul put the fulfillment of this prophecy in the future.

These facts certainly prove that Gary DeMar was in error when he wrote the following:

"***Beyond A.D.70, Israel as a nation plays no prophetic role.****The New Testament only addresses Israel's near destruction never its distant restoration*" [*emphasis added*]. [3]

You Will Be a Blessing

We can also see that in the future Israel will be a blessing to the world:

"*Just as you, Judah and Israel, have been a curse among the nations, so I will save you, and you will be a blessing...This is what the LORD Almighty says: 'In those days ten people from all languages and nations will take firm hold of one Jew by the hem of his robe and say, 'Let us go with you, because we have heard that God is with you'*" (Zech.8:13,23).

It is certain that the Judah and Israel in verse 13 is not referring to the Body of Christ because at no time in history has the Body been a curse among the nations.

End Notes

1. Gary DeMar, *Is Israel's Land Prophetically Significant?*; Accessed November 27, 2018, https://americanvision.org/1731/israels-land-prophetically-significant/

2. Gary DeMar, "'All Israel will be Saved': What it really means," *American Vision*; Accessed 2/2/2019, https://americanvision.org/3902/all-israel-saved-what-it-really-means/

3. Gary DeMar, *Last Days Madness*, 398.

Chapter VI. The Kingdom Age

The Lord Jesus spoke of two different ages, the "age" in which He was then living and an "age to come":

*"'Truly I tell you,' Jesus said to them, 'no one who has left home or wife or brothers or sisters or parents or children for the sake of the kingdom of God will fail to receive many times as much in **this age, and in the age to come eternal life**'"* (Lk. 18:29-30).

*"'Truly I tell you,' Jesus replied, 'no one who has left home or brothers or sisters or mother or father or children or fields for me and the gospel will fail to receive a hundred times as much in **this present age**: homes, brothers, sisters, mothers, children and fields--along with persecutions--**and in the age to come eternal life**"* (Mk. 10:29-30).

The Jews understood that the "age to come" was the kingdom age because they undersood that the kingdom of their promised Messiah would never end--"*in the age to come eternal life*":

*"Of the greatness of his government and peace there will be no end. **He will reign on David's throne and over his kingdom, establishing and upholding it with justice and righteousness from that time on and forever.** The zeal of the LORD Almighty will accomplish this."* (Isa. 9:7).

In the following verse John the Baptist spoke of the kingdom age as being near:

*"In those days John the Baptist came, preaching in the wilderness of Judea and saying, 'Repent, **for the kingdom of heaven has come near**"* (Mt. 13:1-2).

In *The Oxford Dictionary of the Jewish Religion* we read that the term "kingdom of heaven" is "*an eschatological concept referring to a future state of perfection in the world, free from sin and suffering, in which all will live in accordance with the divine will. 'Heaven' is a metonymy for 'God'; the term thus refers not to a heavenly realm but to the kingdom of God on earth."* [1]

In the following verse the Lord Jesus told His disciples to pray for it to come to the earth:

"When ye pray, say, Our Father which art in heaven, Hallowed be thy name. **Thy kingdom come. Thy will be done, as in heaven, so in earth**" (Lk. 11:2).

George Eldon Ladd distinguished between the two ages and recoginized that the age to come is indeed the kingdom age:

"The New Testament sets the Age to Come in direct oppostion to this Age. The present age is evil, but the Kingdom of God belongs to The Age to Come. The Kingdom of God, both as the perfect manifestation of God's reign and the realm of completed blessing, belongs to the The Age to Come." [2]

The World Wide Harvest at the End of the Age

Earlier I quoted the following words of the Lord Jesus where He described what would occur at the "end of the age, the end of the age which will precede the kingdom age:

"He that soweth the good seed is the Son of man; **The field is the world***; the good seed are the children of the kingdom; but the tares are the children of the wicked one; The enemy that sowed them is the devil;* **the harvest is the end of the age (aion)***; and the reapers are the angels. As therefore the tares are gathered and burned in the fire; so shall it be in* **the end of this age (aion)***. The Son of man shall send forth his angels,* **and they shall gather out of his kingdom all things that offend, and them which do iniquity;**

27

And shall cast them into a furnace of fire: there shall be wailing and gnashing of teeth. Then shall the righteous shine forth as the sun in the kingdom of their Father. Who hath ears to hear, let him hear" (Mt. 13:37-43).

At the end of the age in which the Lord Jesus was living when He spoke those words all of the unbelievers will be taken out of that kingdom leaving only believers. The "kingdom" spoken of here is the "universal kingdom" because only that kingdom is made up of both believers and unbelievers:

*"The LORD has established his throne in heaven, and **his kingdom rules over all"*** (Ps. 103:19).

These events will prepare the way for the Messianic kingdom where only those who are born again can enter, as witnessed by the Lord Jesus' words spoken to Nicodemus:

" 'Very truly I tell you, no one can see the kingdom of God unless they are born again....no one can enter the kingdom of God unless they are born of water and the Spirit" (Jn. 3:3,5).

These facts provide overwhelming evidence that the Messianic kingdom has not yet been ushered in and the Lord Jesus is not reigning from the throne of David. That kingdom remains in the future:

" 'The days are coming,' declares the LORD, 'when I will raise up for David a righteous Branch, a King who will reign wisely and do what is just and right in the land'" (Jer. 23:5).

Despite the clear evidence that the Messianic kingdom is not now in existence and therefore the Lord Jesus is not now reigning from David's throne Gary DeMar says the following:

*"Jesus told His disciples that they would see a sign that proved He was in heaven, sitting at His Father's right hand (Acts 2:30-36)...**He now occupies David's throne in the heavenly Jerusalem"*** [emphasis mine]. [3]

Coming or Going?

In the Olivet discourse the disciples asked the Lord Jesus about the sign of His coming so they wanted to know what to expect when He will come or return to the earth:

*"'Tell us,' they said, 'when will this happen, and **what will be the sign of your coming** and of the end of the age?'"* (Mt. 24:3).

In reply the Lord Jesus spoke of the people of the earth seeing him "come" in the clouds of the sky:

*"And then the sign of the Son of Man will appear in the sky, and then all the tribes of the earth will mourn, and they will see the SON OF MAN **COMING** ON THE CLOUDS OF THE SKY with power and great glory"* (Mt. 24:30; NASB).

In regard to this verse Gary DeMar says, *"There is a cloud motif in Scripture. **The reference is found in Daniel 7: 13-14, the passage that Jesus quotes in Matthew 24: 30.** Notice that the coming of the Son of Man in Daniel 7 is not 'down' but 'up'! **The Son of Man, Jesus, comes up 'with the clouds of heaven' to 'the Ancient of Days and was presented before Him'"** [emphasis mine].* [4]

Gary DeMar says that this happened when the Lord Jesus ascended into heaven: *"**At His ascension**, Jesus had come up to the Ancient of Days 'with the cloud of heaven' to receive the kingdom of His Father...the fulfillment of the prophecies regarding a descendant of David's throne forever was realized in Jesus, David's Son"* [emphasis mine] [5]

So according to DeMar the Lord's disciples asked Him the sign of His "coming" or His return to the earth but the Lord Jesus answered them by speaking of His "going" into heaven to receive the kingdom. That makes absolutely no sense because the primary meaning of the Greek word translated "coming" when the Lord's disciples asked Him for the sign of his "coming" is *"the presence of one coming, hence 'the coming, arrival, advent...of a return."* [6]

It is inconceivable that the disciples asked Him about His personal coming or arrival to the earth that He would answer by speaking of His "going" to heaven to receive the kingdom!

Let us look at the passage in regard to the Lord Jesus appearing before the Ancient of Days:

"I saw in the night visions, and, behold, one like the Son of man came with the clouds of heaven, and came to the Ancient of days, and they brought him near before him. And there was given him dominion, and glory, and a kingdom, that all people, nations, and languages, should serve him: his dominion is an everlasting dominion, which shall not pass away, and his kingdom that which shall not be destroyed" (Dan. 7:13-14; KJV).

This passage speaks of the investiture of the Lord Jesus with the kingdom. In other words, this was the act of God in formally giving the Lord Jesus the right of reigning in the kingdom. However, the Lord said that the kingdom will not even be near until He is "seen" coming in a cloud with power and glory:

*" 'People will faint from terror, apprehensive of what is coming on the world, for the heavenly bodies will be shaken. **At that time they will see the Son of Man coming in a cloud with power and great glory.** When these things begin to take place, stand up and lift up your heads, because your redemption is drawing near.' He told them this parable: 'Look at the fig tree and all the trees. When they sprout leaves, you can see for yourselves and know that summer is near. **Even so, when you see these things happening, you know that the kingdom of God is near"*** (Lk. 21:26-31).

The Lord Jesus was given the right to reign in His kingdom when He ascended into heaven but His kingdom will not be operational until He returns to the earth. The same can be said of the throne of David. The angel Gabriel told Mary that the Lord Jesus would be given the throne of David and His kingdom would never end:

"You will conceive and give birth to a son, and you are to call him Jesus. He will be great and will be called the Son of the Most High. **The Lord God will give him the throne of his father David** *and he will reign over Jacob's descendants forever;* **his kingdom will never end**" (Lk. 31:34).

The throne of David was promised to the Lord Jesus but didn't receive possession of it until He ascended into heaven. But He will not begin to sit upon that throne and reign until He returns to the earth, as witnessed by His words here:

"When the Son of man shall come in his glory, and all the holy angels with him, **then shall he sit upon the throne of his glory**" (Mt. 25:31; KJV).

Here the Lord tells us that it will be "then,"when He comes to the earth when He will sit upon His throne, the throne of David. The Greek word translated "then" means "*of things future: 'then'...when the things under discussion take place.*" [7]

So it will not be until He "comes" to the earth that He will sit upon the throne of David. The meaning of the Greek word translated "come" in this verse is the same meaning for the word when the Lord's disciples asked Him the following question:

" *'Tell us,' they said, 'when will this happen, and what will be the sign of your* **coming** *and of the end of the age?* '" (Mt. 24:3).

Again, the meaning of that Greek word is "*the presence of one coming, hence 'the coming, arrival, advent...of a return.*" [8]

Not only that, but at Acts 7:55 and at Revelation 5:6 the Lord Jesus is seen in heaven and in both instances He is seen standing and not sitting on any throne. In fact, in the passages at Revelation 4 and 5 the Apostle John describes many things which he saw around the throne of God and he made no mention of the throne of David. Therefore at those points in time He is not reigning in His kingdom even though the

Scriptures state that His kingdom shall never end. From these facts we can understand that when the Lord Jesus ascended into heaven He was formally given the possession of the kingdom and the throne of David but He will not begin to sit upon that throne and reign in His kingdom until He returns to the earth.

The Present Evil Age

The Preterist's teaching about the Last Days is totally dependent on the idea that we are now living during the kingdom age despite the fact that Paul calls the present age an "evil" age:

*"Grace and peace to you from God our Father and the Lord Jesus Christ, who gave himself for our sins to rescue us from **the present evil age**"* (Gal. 1:3-4).

It is difficult to imagine a teaching as absurd and grotesque as this perversion of the Holy Scriptures put forth by the Preterists. However, the idea that even though the disciples asked the Lord about His "coming" to the earth He answered by speaking of His "going" to heaven comes close!

End Notes

1. *The Oxford Dictionary of the Jewish Religion*, ed. Adele Berlin (New York, NY: Oxford University Press, 2011), 428.

2. George Eldon Ladd, *The Gospel of the Kingdom* (Grand Rapids: Wm. Eerdmans Publishing Company, 1959), 31.

3. Gary DeMar, *Last Days Madness*, 165.

4. *Ibid.*, 161.

5. *Ibid.*, 163, 165.

6. Joseph Henry Thayer, *A Greek-English Lexicon of the New Testament*, 490.

7. *Ibid.*, 629.

8. *Ibid.*, 490.

Chapter VII. The Kingdom Age
Part 2

The Tabernacle of David

Once again, Gary DeMar wrote that the Lord Jesus now occupies David's throne in the heavenly Jerusalem:

*"Jesus told His disciples that they would see a sign that proved He was in heaven, sitting at His Father's right hand (Acts 2:30-36)...**He now occupies David's throne in the heavenly Jerusalem**"* [emphasis mine]. [1]

Let us look at the following prophecy which will be fulfilled by the Lord Jesus Christ:

*"In that day will **I raise up again the tabernacle of David that is fallen down; and I will build again the ruins thereof, and I will set it up**...That the residue of men might seek after the Lord, and all the Gentiles, upon whom my name is called, saith the Lord, who does all these things"* (Amos 9:11-12; *Septuagint*).

As soon as David became king of Israel he sought to bring the Ark of the Covenant back to the people so he raised up a tabernacle or tent where he could place the Ark:

*"After David had constructed buildings for himself in the City of David, **he prepared a place for the ark of God and pitched a tent for it**"* (1 Chron. 15:1).

It will be in the Tabernacle of David where the Lord Jesus will reign from his throne:

*"And in mercy **shall the throne be established: and He shall sit upon it in truth in the tabernacle of David**, judging, and seeking judgment, and hasting righteousness"* (Isa. 16:5;

KJV).

Now let us look at the following prophecy again:

"*In that day will I raise up again the tabernacle of David that is fallen down; and I will build again the ruins thereof, and I will set it up*" (Amos 9:11-12; *Septuagint*).

This prophecy will be fulfilled when the Lord Jesus restores the house or family of David by ruling from the throne of David. It will happen "in that day." Later, at the Jerusalem council at Acts 15, James quotes Amos 9:11-12 and makes a change to that prophecy (in 'bold') and by that change we can know that the Lord Jesus will not raise up again the tabernacle of David and sit upon the throne of David until He returns to the earth:

"**After this I will return and rebuild David's fallen tent.** *Its ruins I will rebuild, and I will restore it*" (Acts 15:16).

The Lord Jesus will not sit upon the throne of David until the tabernacle of David is raised up again and that will not happen until He returns to the earth. This is more evidence that Gary DeMar is in error when he teaches that the Lord Jesus is now sitting upon the throne of David and that the Messianic Kingdom already exists.

His Appearance And His Kingdom

Paul taught that the Lord Jesus' kingdom remained in the future when he wrote the following:

"*I charge thee therefore before God, and **the Lord Jesus Christ, who shall judge the quick and the dead at his appearing and his kingdom**" (2 Tim. 4:1;KJV).

Here we see that Paul places the kingdom age in the future at the appearing of the Lord Jesus when He will judge the living and the dead. In the following verse Paul speaks of the judgment of the living at the Lord Jesus' appearance:

*"God is just: He will pay back trouble to those who trouble you and give relief to you who are troubled, and to us as well. This will happen when the Lord Jesus is revealed from heaven in blazing fire with his powerful angels. **He will punish those who do not know God and do not obey the gospel of our Lord Jesus**"* (2 Thess. 1:6-8).

Besides that, while the Lord walked the earth He spoke of a future judgment of those in the grave:

"...a time is coming when all who are in their graves will hear his voice and come out--those who have done what is good will rise to live, and those who have done what is evil will rise to be condemned" (Jn. 5:28-29).

The Lord Jesus has been given all authority to judge (v. 27) and He will judge who will be raised to eternal life on the last day, the last day which will precede the kingdom age:

*"For my Father's will is that everyone who looks to the Son and believes in him shall have eternal life, **and I will raise them up at the last day**"* (Jn. 6:40).

The words of Paul about the time when the kingdom will be set up on the earth directly contradict the teaching of Gary DeMar that the Lord Jesus is now reigning from the Davidic throne.

My Kingdom Is Not of This World

When the Lord Jesus walked the earth He said the following about His Kingdom:

*"**My kingdom is not of this world**. If My kingdom were of this world, then My servants would be fighting so that I would not be handed over to the Jews; **but as it is, My kingdom is not of this realm**"* (Jn. 18:36; NASB).

Gary DeMar writes that *"when Jesus said that His kingdom is not 'of' this world, He means that it does not 'derive its authority and power from' the world. As He* *added, His kingdom is from another place. **This verse refers to the 'origin' of the kingdom, not to a restriction of where it operates**" [emphasis added]. ²*

DeMar says that this verse refers to the "origin" of the kingdom. However, the "origin" of the kingdom of which the Lord Jesus speaks is the earth because the location of the throne of that kingdom (the throne of David) is the earth:

"So Solomon sat on the throne of his father David, and his rule was firmly established" (1 Ki. 2:12).

Of course the location of the throne of any kingdom defines the location of the kingdom. Since the location of the throne of David is the earth then we can know that the location of the kingdom in view is also the earth. The angel Gabriel told Mary that her Son will be given the throne of David:

*"You will conceive and give birth to a son, and you are to call him Jesus. He will be great and will be called the Son of the Most High. **The Lord God will give him the throne of his father David**, and he will reign over Jacob's descendants forever; his kingdom will never end"* (Lk. 1:21-23).

The Kingdom of God is in Your Midst

Let us look at the words of the Lord Jesus in the following verse:

*"The coming of the kingdom of God is not something that can be observed, nor will people say, 'Here it is,' or 'There it is,' because **the kingdom of God is in your midst**"* (Lk. 17:21).

In His commentary on this verse DeMar writes the following:

"Moreover, in Luke 17:21, Jesus tells the Pharisees that the 'Kingdom of God is within you.' The Greek word for 'within' can also mean 'in your midst.' Since the Pharisees

*were not believers, the better translation seems to be 'in your midst.' Whatever it means, one thing is clear: **Jesus was announcing that God's kingdom was present, not exclusively future**" [emphasis added].* [3]

When the Lord spoke of the kingdom being in the midst He was using figurative language which is called "Metonymy," and in this instance it is specifically referred to in the following way: "*Of the Subject. When the subject is put for something pertaining to it.*" [4]

S. Vernon McCasland writes that "*Metonymy is an exchange of names between things related. It is founded not on resemblance but on relation of ...place and inhabitant...*" [5]

Since the Jews who heard the Lord Jesus say that the kingdom was in their midst knew that the environment in which they were living eliminated the idea that the promised kingdom was actually in their midst (Dan. 7:14) they would realize that the Lord was using figurative language to declare, in a subtle manner, that their promised King was in their midst.

After all, if the kingdom was already their midst, why would He tell His disciples to pray for it to come upon the earth?

"*This, then, is how you should pray: 'Our Father in heaven, hallowed be your name, your kingdom come, your will be done, on earth as it is in heaven*'" (Mt. 6:9-10).

Does the Lord Jesus Occupy David's Throne in Heaven?

Gary Demar writes that "*Jesus occupies David's throne in heaven (Acts 2:29--36).*" [6]

At Acts 2:33 Peter ties what he said at Acts 2:33 to Psalm 110:

"*Exalted to the right hand of God, he has received from the Father the promised Holy Spirit and has poured out what* *you now see and hear. For David did not ascend to heaven, and yet he said,'**The Lord said to my Lord: Sit at my right hand until I make your enemies a footstool for your feet.** "* (Acts 2:33-35).

If Peter was telling his listeners that the Lord Jesus is now sitting on David's throne in heaven he certainly would have never quoted anything from Psalm 110 because that psalm places Him at the right hand of the Father prior to His kingdom becoming operative:

"The LORD says to my lord: 'Sit at my right hand until I make your enemies a footstool for your feet'...The Lord is at your right hand ; he will crush kings on the day of his wrath. ***He will judge the nations, heaping up the dead and crushing the rulers of the whole earth*** *"* (Ps. 110:1,5-6).

Before the kingdom will be ushered in the LORD will take out all of the unbelievers on the face of the earth:

"I looked, and there before me was a white cloud, and seated on the cloud was one like a son of man with a crown of gold on his head and a sharp sickle in his hand. Then another angel came out of the temple and called in a loud voice to him who was sitting on the cloud, 'Take your sickle and reap, because the time to reap has come, for the harvest of the earth is ripe.' So he who was seated on the cloud swung his sickle over the earth, and the earth was harvested" (Rev. 14:14-16).

It will be then when the Lord Jesus will crush kings on the day of his wrath and will judge the nations, heaping up the dead and crushing the rulers of the whole earth. That will leave only those who are "born again" to populate the kingdom:

"Jesus replied, 'Very truly I tell you, no one can see the kingdom of God unless they are born again...no one can enter the kingdom of God unless they are born of water and the Spirit.'" (Jn. 3:3,5).

End Notes

1. Gary DeMar, *Last Days Madness*, 165.

2. Gary DeMar, *Myths, Lies, & Half Truths* (Powder Springs, GA: American Vision, 2004), 207.

3. Gary DeMar, *"The Kingdom Has Come"*, The American Vision; Accessed December 12, 2018, https://americanvision.org/1718/kingdom-has-come/

4. E. W. Bullinger, *Figures of Speech used in the Bible*; Accessed December 12, 2018, https://levendwater.org/companion/append6.html

5. S. Vernon McCasland, *Some New Testament Metonyms For God*; Accessed December 12, 2018, https://www.jstor.org/stable/3261996?seq=1#page_sc an_tab_contents

6. Gary DeMar, "Is Jesus Going to Reign on Earth?" *The American Vision*; Accessed December 27, 2018, https://americanvision.org/5141/is-jesus-going-to-reign-on-earth/

Chapter VIII. Will the Kingdom be Restored to Israel?

The Apostles were with the resurrected Lord Jesus for forty days while He spoke about the kingdom:

*"To whom also he shewed himself alive after his passion by many infallible proofs, being seen of them forty days, and **speaking of the things pertaining to the kingdom of God***" (Acts 1:3).

Certainly the Apostles would know the most basic things about the kingdom and they believed that it would be "restored to Israel." They asked Him:

*"When they therefore were come together, they asked of him, saying, Lord, **wilt thou at this time restore again the kingdom to Israel?**"* (Acts 1:6).

The Apostles would be aware of the prophecies that speak of a time in the future when the Lord Jesus would reign from the throne of David and Israel will live in safety:

*" 'The days are coming,' declares the LORD, 'when **I will raise up for David a righteous Branch, a King who will reign** wisely and do what is just and right in the land. **In his days Judah will be saved and Israel will live in safety**"* (Jer. 23:5-6).

The Lord only answered by saying that they were not to know the time when it would happen:

"And he said unto them, It is not for you to know the times or the seasons, which the Father hath put in his own power" (Acts 1:7).

Gary DeMar makes the following remarks about the Apostle's question concerning the kingdom:

"...it is obvious from the apostles' question in Acts 1:6 that they believed the kingdom had been taken from Israel, because they ask, 'Lord, is it at this time You are restoring the kingdom to Israel?'" [1]

Then he says the following about that kingdom:

"If the kingdom is defined in political terms, where Jesus personally and physically rules from Jerusalem in the midst of a rebuilt temple, a renewed sacrificial system, and the reestablishment of the Old Testament theocratic government, then God's kingdom has not yet come...This view of the kingdom is advocated by dispensational premillennialists who assert that Jesus offered to Israel a physical, political, earthly kingdom, but the Jews rejected Jesus as their king, thus initiating the kingdom's 'postponement.' Such a view contradicts Scripture."

Earthly Kingdom

Yes, dispensational premillennialists believe that the kingdom which will be restored to Israel will be an earthly kingdom because of the following prophecy I quoted earlier:

*" 'The days are coming,' declares the LORD, 'when I will raise up for David a righteous Branch, a King who will reign wisely and do what is just and right **in the land. In his days Judah will be saved and Israel will live in safety**"* (Jer. 23:5-6).

The Kingdom Under Solomon

Since the Apostles asked the Lord about a "restored" kingdom then we must examine the make-up of that kingdom when Solomon ruled from the throne of David. From the very beginning the throne of David was established as an earthly throne because Solomon sat upon that throne on the earth:

"So Solomon sat on the throne of his father David, and his rule was firmly established" (1 Ki. 2:12).

According to the promise which God made to David the earthly temple and his earthly throne were established for ever:

*"**Your house** and your kingdom will endure forever before me ; **your throne will be established forever**"* (2 Sam. 7:16).

Since both the earthly temple and the earthly throne had been established forever then there will never be a time when the throne of David will be anything other than an earthly throne. By the words of the Prophet Haggai we can see what might be described as a "principle of continuity" in the history of the temple. The temple that stood at the time of the Lord could be leveled to the ground and then be rebuilt and still be considered the same temple. The prophet Haggai revealed that at the time of the rebuilding of the temple after it had been destroyed it remained the same temple:

"Who of you is left who saw this house in its former glory?" (Hag. 2:3).

So a rebuilt temple can be considered a continuation of the two preceding temples according to the Scriptures. Therefore any future temple will not have to be rebuilt with the same stones as was the temple standing when the Lord Jesus walked the earth in order to be considered the same temple.

Besides that, the LORD also said that He would not "alter" the promises which He made to David:

*"I have made a covenant with my chosen one, **I have sworn to David my servant**...I will not take my love from him, nor will I ever betray my faithfulness. I will not violate my covenant **or alter what my lips have uttered**. Once for all, I have sworn by my holiness--and I will not lie to David"* (Ps. 89:3,33-35).

According to Gary DeMar the LORD changed the earthly throne of David into a heavenly throne despite the fact that He said that He would not alter the promises which He made to David:

*"Jesus told His disciples that they would see a sign that proved He was in heaven, sitting at His Father's right hand (Acts 2:30-36)...**He now occupies David's throne in the heavenly Jerusalem**"* [emphasis mine]. [2]

There is even more evidence that in the future the Lord Jesus' throne will be on the earth. The prophet Ezekiel says that the LORD brought him to the *"**land of Israel**"* (Ez.40:2) and was placed on a high mountain where he saw a structure like a city on the south. Then he was brought to a "temple" (41:1) and its "inner court" (43:5) where the LORD said the following to him:

*"Son of man, **this is the place of my throne** and the place for the soles of my feet. **This is where I will live among the Israelites forever**"* (Ez. 43:7).

Again, Gary DeMar said that if the Lord Jesus physically rules from Jerusalem in the midst of a rebuilt temple then God's kingdom has not yet come. The facts prove that the Messianic kingdom remains in the future.

The Kingdom of God Will Be Taken Away From You

Gary Demar writes that *"Israel had the kingdom, **an extension of the Old Testament kingdom**, therefore, it was a present reality: 'The kingdom of God will be taken away from you, and given to a nation producing the fruit of it.' Jesus could not take away from them what they did not have* [emphasis added]. [3]

First of all, I have just demonstrated that the Israelites have not yet received "an extension of the Old Testament kingdom" so DeMar's argument falls apart from the beginning. Here is the passage which he has in view:

*"Jesus said to them, 'Have you never read in the Scriptures:' 'The stone the builders rejected has become the cornerstone; the Lord has done this, and it is marvelous in our eyes'? '***Therefore I tell you that the kingdom of God will be taken away from you and given to a people who will produce its fruit.*** Anyone who falls on this stone will be broken to pieces; anyone on whom it falls will be crushed.' When the chief priests and the Pharisees heard Jesus' parables, they knew he was talking about them"* (Mt. 21:42-45).

The "kingdom of God" to which the Lord Jesus made reference in this passage is the Universal Kingdom spoken of in this verse:

"The LORD has established his throne in heaven, and his kingdom rules over all" (Ps.103:9).

The "kingdom of God" was given to the nation of Israel in the sense that she was to be a channel of blessing to the world, and one of the duties assigned to that nation was the stewardship to be a witness to the fact of the existence of God and that there is only one God:

*"**Ye are my witnesses***, saith the LORD, and my servant whom I have chosen: that ye may know and believe me, and understand that I am he: before me there was no God formed, neither shall there be after me. I, even I, am the LORD; and beside me there is no saviour. I have declared, and have saved, and I have shewed, when there was no strange god among you: therefore **ye are my witnesses**, saith the LORD, that I am God"* (Isa. 43:10-12).

The Jews were given the oracles of God (Ro.3:2) and it was through the nation of Israel that the rest of the world would come to the knowledge of God:

"Thus saith the LORD of hosts; In those days it shall come to pass, that ten men shall take hold out of all languages of the nations, even shall take hold of the skirt of

him that is a Jew, saying, We will go with you: for we have heard that God is with you" (Zech. 8:23).

While He walked the earth the Lord Jesus said that "*salvation is of the Jews*" (Jn. 4:22).

Because the chief priests and Pharisees rejected their promised Messiah and the nation crucified Him the responsibilty of the universal kingdom of God was given to the little flock who did in fact produce fruit by proclaiming that the Lord Jesus is the Christ, the Son of God.

"*Then Jesus said to his disciples...Do not be afraid, little flock, for your Father has been pleased to give you the kingdom*" (Lk. 12:22,32).

End Notes

1. Gary DeMar, "Whose Kingdom is It?" *The Americal Vision*; Accessed December 22, 2018, https://americanvision.org/1716/whose-kingdom/

2. Gary DeMar, *Last Days Madness*, 165.

3. Gary DeMar, *Myths, Lies, & Half Truths* [Powder Springs, GA: American Vision, 2004], 223.

Chapter IX. The Return of the Lord Jesus to the Earth

At the time the Lord Jesus ascended up to heaven His disciples were told the following about His return to the earth:

"Which also said, Ye men of Galilee, why stand ye gazing up into heaven? this same Jesus, which is taken up from you into heaven, **shall so come in like manner as ye have seen him go into heaven.** *Then returned they unto Jerusalem from* **the mount called Olivet**, *which is from Jerusalem a sabbath day's journey"* (Acts 1:11-12).

In his commentary on these verse S. Lewis Johnson wrote, *"And so how will Jesus come again? Well, look at it for a moment and think about it. He went up personally. He will come back personally. He went up in bodily form -- glorified bodily form, but bodily form. He will come back in glorified bodily form. He went up in visible form. He will come back in visible form.* **He went up from a particular place, the Mount of Olives. He will come back --Zechariah tells us--to a particular place, the Mount of Olives"** [*emphasis added*]. [1]

Yes, when the Lord Jesus returns to the earth He will fulfill the following prophecy of Zechariah and in that day His feet shall stand on the Mount of Olives:

"For I will gather all nations against Jerusalem to battle; and the city shall be taken, and the houses rifled, and the women ravished; and half of the city shall go forth into captivity, and the residue of the people shall not be cut off from the city. **Then shall the LORD go forth, and fight against those nations, as when he fought in the day of battle. And his feet shall stand in that day upon the mount**

of Olives, which is before Jerusalem on the east" (Zech. 14:2-4).

John Walvoord wrote that *"**The great tribulation**...is a specific period of time beginning with the abomination of desolation **and closing with the second coming of Christ"** [emphasis added]* [2]

Yes, the Lord Jesus will return at the end of the great tribulation and rescue His people at the time of their greatest peril. Let us look at the events leading up to the the great tribulation:

*"When ye therefore shall see **the abomination of desolation**, spoken of by Daniel the prophet, stand in the holy place...Then let them which be in Judaea flee into the mountains...But pray ye that your flight be not in the winter, neither on the sabbath day: For then shall be **great tribulation**, such as was not since the beginning of the world to this time, no, nor ever shall be. **And except those days should be shortened, there should no flesh be saved: but for the elect's sake those days shall be shortened"** (Mt. 24:15-22).

First the abomination of desolation will stand in the holy place and then "there shall be great tribulation." Then we read that the tribulation will be shortened and that will happen when the Lord Jesus returns to the earth and fights against all the nations which will come against Jerusalem (Zech.14:1-3). This is the only place in the Lord's timeline where the prophecy of Zechariah 14:1-4 can be fulfilled because it takes place before the Lord Jesus begins to reign as King (Zech. 14:9).

However, when we look at the same timeline outlined by the Lord Jesus concerning these events it appears that the Lord Jesus will not return until AFTER the great tribulation:

"But immediately after the tribulation of those days the sun shall be darkened, and the moon shall not give her light, and the stars shall fall from heaven, and the powers of the heavens shall be shaken:and then the sign of the Son of Man

will appear in the sky. Then all the tribes of the earth will mourn, and they will see the Son of Man coming on the clouds of the sky with power and great glory" (Mt. 24:29-30).

How can this be reconciled with the fact that the Lord Jesus will return at the end of the great tribulation and not after the great tribulation is over? When the Lord spoke of the "sign" of the Son of Man appearing in the sky at Matthew 24:30 His words were in answer to the disciple's question concerning the "sign" of His coming which will not happen until the end of the age:

"*As Jesus was sitting on the Mount of Olives, the disciples came to him privately. 'Tell us,' they said, 'when will this happen, and **what will be the sign of your coming and of the end of the age**'*" (Mt. 24:3)

Therefore, we can understand that when all of the tribes of the earth see Him in the sky that will be a "sign" of His coming which will occur at the end of the age. And the end of the age will not happen until all the unbelievers will be weeded out of the world (Mt.13:37-43). The event when the Lord Jesus' feet will stand on the Mount of Olives will precede the events concerning the end of the age.

In *The Bible Knowledge Commentary* Louis Barbieri, Jr., wrote: "*Exactly what the sign of the Son of Man will be is unknown...the sign may be the lightening, **or perhaps the Lord Himself**" [emphasis added]. [3]*

Now let us look at the following verse again:

"*But immediately after the tribulation of those days the sun shall be darkened, and the moon shall not give her light, and the stars shall fall from heaven, and the powers of the heavens shall be shaken: and then the sign of the Son of Man will appear in the sky. Then all the tribes of the earth will mourn, and they will see the Son of Man coming on the clouds of the sky with power and great glory*" (Mt. 24:29-30).

According to this passage the Lord Jesus will be seen in the sky after the sun and the moon will be darkened. The following verse speaks of those same signs and the same appearance of the Lord Jesus and from this prophecy we know that He will be departing from Jerusalem when He will be seen in the sky:

"The sun and the moon shall be darkened, and the stars shall withdraw their shining. The LORD also shall roar out of Zion, and utter his voice from Jerusalem; and the heavens and the earth shall shake: but the LORD will be the hope of his people, and the strength of the children of Israel" (Joel 3:15-16).

To summarize, the Lord Jesus appearance spoken of at Zechariah 14:2-4 will precede His coming which will happen at the end of the age. Then after He rescues His people at the end of the great tribulation then there will be signs seen in the sky. Now let us look at the following verse again:

"But immediately after the tribulation of those days the sun shall be darkened, and the moon shall not give her light, and the stars shall fall from heaven, and the powers of the heavens shall be shaken: **and then the sign of the Son of Man will appear in the sky**. *Then all the tribes of the earth will mourn, and they will see the Son of Man coming on the clouds of the sky with power and great glory"* (Mt. 24:29-30).

The Greek word translated "then" at the beginning of verse 30 does not always mean that the things spoken of as occuring will happen immediately. The word also means *"of things future ; 'then' (at length) when the things under discussion takes place."* [4]

This is the correct meaning of the word because the Lord Jesus speaks of this coming at the end of the age in the following way:

" As it was in the days of Noah, so it will be at the coming of the Son of Man. For in the days before the flood, people were eating and drinking, marrying and giving in marriage,

up to the day Noah entered the ark; and they knew nothing about what would happen until the flood came and took them all away. That is how it will be at the coming of the Son of Man. Two men will be in the field; one will be taken and the other left. Two women will be grinding with a hand mill; one will be taken and the other left. **Therefore keep watch, because you do not know on what day your Lord will come"** (Mt. 24:37-42).

If the coming of the Lord Jesus which is the sign of his coming at the end of the age (v.30) is to follow immediately after the signs will appear in the sky then it would make no sense for the Lord Jesus to say that no one will know the day of that coming of the Lord Jesus. Therefore, we can understand that the Lord Jesus will return to the earth and in that day He will rescue His people at the end of the great tribulation. Then immediately after that signs will be seen in the sky. The Lord will remain in Jerusalem during the time when the judgments spoken of in the book of Revelation are fulfilled (Seven Seals, Seven Trumpet Judgments, and the Seven Vial Judgments) and then He will roar out of Jerusalem and will be victorious at the battle of Armagedden (Rev. 16:13-16, 19, 17-21).

So we can know that when the Lord Jesus returns to the earth He will fulfill the prophecy at Zechariah 14 and therefore we know that no one will be caught up when the Lord Jesus descends from heaven. That is because it will not be until after the great tribulation is over and the Lord Jesus roars out of Jerusalem when the saints will be gathered together:

"But in those days, **after that tribulation,** *the sun shall be darkened, and the moon shall not give her light, And the stars of heaven shall fall, and the powers that are in heaven shall be shaken. And then shall they see the Son of man coming in the clouds with great power and glory.* **And then shall he send his angels, and shall gather together his elect from the four winds, from the uttermost part of the earth to the uttermost part of heaven"** (Mk. 13:24-27).

If the saints are caught up to meet the Lord Jesus in the air when He descends from heaven while returning to the earth then there would be no need for the angels to gather together the elect because the elect would have already met the Lord Jesus in the air:

*"Then we which are alive and remain shall be caught up together with them in the clouds, **to meet the Lord in the air**"* (1 Thess. 4:17).

It is impossible that the "catching up" of the saints mentioned at 1 Thessalonians 4:17 can happen at the time of the Lord Jesus' return to the earth when His feet shall stand on the Mount of Olives.

End Notes

1. S. Lewis Johnson, *The Plan and the Power and the Promise*, Accessed June 6, 2018. http://sljinstitute.net/acts/the-plan-the-power-and-the-promise/

2. John F. Walvoord *The Signs of the End of the Age*, Accessed June 8, 2018. https://bible.org/seriespage/24-signs-end-age

3. Louis Barbieri, Jr., "Matthew" in *The Bible Knowledge Commentary; NewTestament*, 78.

4. Joseph Henry Thayer, *A Greek-English Lexicon of the New Testament*, 629.

X. Timing Is Everything

Gary DeMar writes that *"One of the first things a Christian must learn in interpreting the Bible is to pay attention to the time texts"*. He says that futurists *"ignore the time texts that speak of a near coming of Jesus in judgment upon an apostate Judaism that rejected its Messiah in the first century"* [1]

Gary DeMar overlooks the fact that on more than one occasion the promises of God were delayed or postponed. For instance, from the beginning of the Lord Jesus' ministry He proclaimed that the kingdom had come "near":

*"From that time on Jesus began to preach, **'Repent, for the kingdom of heaven has come near'**"* (Mt. 4:17; NIV).

In *The Scofield Study Bible* we read that *"the Biblical term 'at hand' or 'near' is never a positive affirmation that the person or thing said to be at hand will immediately appear, but only that person or thing has the quality of imminency."* [2]

After the leaders of the nation of Israel plotted His death the Lord Jesus told His disciples not to make Him known:

*"**But the Pharisees went out and plotted how they might kill Jesus**. Aware of this, Jesus withdrew from that place. A large crowd followed him, and he healed all who were ill. **He warned them not to tell others about him**"* (Mt. 12:14-16).

Due to the actions of the leaders of Israel the coming of the kingdom was delayed. Later the Lord Jesus said that the kingdom would only be near when He returns to earth:

*"**At that time they will see the Son of Man coming in a cloud with power and great glory.** When these things begin to take place, stand up and lift up your heads, because your*

*redemption is drawing near.' He told them this parable: 'Look at the fig tree and all the trees. When they sprout leaves, you can see for yourselves and know that summer is near. Even so, **when you see these things happening, you know that the kingdom of God is near**'"* (Lk. 21:27-31).

It will not be until the Lord Jesus returns to the earth in a cloud with power and glory that the kingdom will be near. In Chapter V it has been proven that the kingdom age has not yet been ushered in so it remains in the future--when the Lord Jesus returns to the earth.

The Rapture

The word "rapture" comes from the Latin Translation of the Greek word translated "caught up" in the following verse:

*"After that, we who are still alive and are left will be **caught up** together with them in the clouds to meet the Lord in the air. And so we will be with the Lord forever"* (1 Thess. 4:17; NIV).

*"deinde nos qui vivimus qui relinquimur simul **rapiemur** cum illis in nubibus obviam Domino in aera et sic semper cum Domino erimus"* (1 Thess. 4:17; Latin Vulgate).

The following verse speaks of the same event when living saints will be "caught up" to meet the Lord Jesus in the air:

*"But our citizenship is in heaven. **And we eagerly await a Savior from there, the Lord Jesus Christ**, who, by the power that enables him to bring everything under his control, **will transform our lowly bodies so that they will be like his glorious body"** (Phil. 3:20-21).

The Lord Jesus' Appearance is Near

In the following passage from the book of James we read

that the believers were taught that the Lord Jesus' appearance when they will be caught up and put on new glorious bodies like His glorious body is near:

*"You too, be patient and stand firm, because **the Lord's coming is near.** Don't grumble against one another, brothers and sisters, or you will be judged. **The Judge is standing at the door!"** (Jas. 5:8-9).*

The Greek word translated "is near" at James 5:8 is *eggizo* and in this verse that word means *"to be imminent."* [3]

When we combine James 5:9 with the one which precedes it we see a twofold revelation of imminency in regard to the coming of the Lord. What cannot be missed is the fact that the phrase *"The Judge is standing at the door"* (referring to the "judgment seat of Christ") reinforces the idea that the coming of the Lord is "near" in time and both verses speak of an imminent coming of the Lord Jesus.

So at James 5:8-9 we see a double revelation of imminency in regard to the coming of the Lord. In these two verses the Apostle James employs a literary device, specifically a figure of speech called *Pleonasm*, which is defined in the following way:

"When what is said is, immediately after, put in another or opposite way to make it impossible for the sense to be missed." [4]

With these things in mind we can understand that the first century Christians were taught that the Lord could appear at any moment.

The Redemption of Our Body

An examination of another "timing" passages reveals that the Apostle Paul used a Greek word in regard to the Lord's appearing that can only mean that His appearing could occur at any moment:

*"But our citizenship is in heaven. And we **eagerly await (apekdechomai)** a Savior from there, the Lord Jesus Christ, who, by the power that enables him to bring everything under his control, **will transform our lowly bodies so that they will be like his glorious body**"* (Phil. 3:20-21).

One of the meanings of the Greek word *apekdechomai* is *"to look for, expect, wait for, await."* [5]

Vine's Dictionary gives the meaning of how the word is used at Phiippians 3:20 as *"expect eagerly."* [6]

If the Lord's appearance spoken of at Philippians 3:20 is the same one which will not happen until after the abomination of desolation stands in the holy place (Mt.24:15-30) then Paul would not have used a word which means to "expect eagerly" because no one would be "eagerly" expecting that appearance until the abomination of desolation stands in the holy place.

In the following passage Paul uses another Greek word to describe the attitude believers should have about the appearance of the Lord Jesus at the rapture, when they will experience the redemption of their new, glorified bodies:

*"For I reckon that the sufferings of this present time are not worthy to be compared with **the glory which shall be revealed in us**. For the **earnest expectation (apokaradokia)** of the creature waiteth for the manifestation of the sons of God...And not only they, but ourselves also, which have the firstfruits of the Spirit, even we ourselves groan within ourselves, waiting for the adoption, that is, **the redemption of our body**"* (Ro. 8:18,19,23).

Here Paul is speaking of *"the redemption of our body,"* an event that will happen when the Lord Jesus appears. The Greek word translated "earnest expectation" is *"apokaradokia"*, and this word means *"to watch with head erect or outstretched...to wait for in suspense."* [7]

Vine's Dictionary of New Testament Words says that the word means *"primarily 'a watching with outstretched head' (apo, 'from,' kara, 'the head,' and dokeo, 'to look, to watch'), signifies "strained expectancy, eager longing," the stretching forth of the head indicating an 'expectation' of something from a certain place, Rom. 8:19; Phil. 1:20."* [8]

The same Greek word *"was used in Greek writings to describe the alert watchman who peered into the darkness, eagerly looking for the first gleam of the distant beacon which would announce the capture of Troy."* [9]

So according to the Greek experts the word that Paul used in regard to the "redemption of our body" is a word that indicates that this event can take place at any moment. That can only mean that the following verses, which speak of the Lord Jesus' return to the earth, cannot be the same imminent coning of the Lord because before He can return to the earth the abomination of desolation must first stand in the holy place:

"When ye therefore shall see the abomination of desolation, spoken of by Daniel the prophet, stand in the holy place...Then let them which be in Judaea flee into the mountains...For then shall be great tribulation, such as was not since the beginning of the world to this time, no, nor ever shall be...And then shall appear the sign of the Son of man in heaven: and then shall all the tribes of the earth mourn, and they shall see the Son of man coming in the clouds of heaven with power and great glory" (Mt. 24:15-16, 21, 30; KJV).

In other words, the Apostle Paul would not have told anyone to be looking for the appearance of the Lord Jesus with an expectation of seeing Him at any moment if He could not possibly appear until after the unfulfilled prophecy of the abomination of desolation standing in the holy place is fulfilled.

The Long Delay of the Return of Christ

Sir Robert Anderson uses the unfaithfulness of Israel to

explain the delay of the blessing hope, the time when Christians will be caught up to meet the Lord Jesus in the air:

"Israel's story may teach us something here. When the people were encamped at Sinai, Canaan lay but a few days' march across the desert. And in the second year from the Exodus, they were led to the borders of the land, and bidden to enter and take possession of it. 'But they entered not in because of unbelief'...Does not this throw light on the seeming failure of 'the hope of the Church'? Putting from us the profane thought that the Lord has been unmindful of His promise, are we not led to the conclusion that this long delay has been due to the unfaithfulness of His people upon earth?" [10]

Anderson also says: *"Though the purposes of God cannot be thwarted by the sins of men, the fulfilment of them may be thus postponed. And just as the wilderness apostasy of Israel prolonged their wanderings for forty years, although Canaan was but a few days' march from Sinai, so the far more gross apostasy of Christendom has prolonged for nigh two thousand years an era which the Lord and His Apostles taught the early saints to look upon as brief."* [11]

The Unfaithfulness in the Early Church

Dr. Merle D'Aubigne', author of the *History of the Reformation in the Sixteenth Century*, writes the following in his Introduction to Ranke's *History of the Popes*:

"The evangelical, which is the primitive system, extends only to the commencement of the second century. Then the word of God reigned supreme, and a living faith in the grace which that word proclaims, was regarded as entirely sufficient for saving the sinner; **but at the commencement of the second century the void left in the Church by the death of the apostles, and the invasion of the house of God by the human element, brought about a general alteration in the**

spirit and organisation of the Church, and a great crisis ensued" [*emphasis added*]. [12]

This great crisis which began in the second century when those in the church began to adopt the things of demon-worship from the various pagan religions into the church. John Henry Cardinal Newman sums up that development in the following way:

*"Confiding then in the power of Christianity to resist the infection of evil, and **to transmute the very instruments and appendages of demon-worship to an evangelical use**, and feeling also that these usages had originally come from primitive revelations and from the instinct of nature, though they had been corrupted; and that they must invent what they needed, if they did not use what they found; and that they were moreover possessed of the very archetypes, of which paganism attempted the shadows; **the rulers of the Church from early times were prepared, should the occasion arise, to adopt, or imitate, or sanction the existing rites and customs of the populace, as well as the philosophy of the educated class"** [*emphasis added*]. [13]*

Cardinal Newman failed to mention that one of the things of the pagan religions which was adopted into the early church was the teaching of baptismal regeneration, spoken of here by Justin Martyr (100-165), less than fifty years after the death of the last Apostle, John:

*"And this food is called among us the Eucharist, of which no one is allowed to partake but the man who believes that the things which we teach are true, and **who has been washed with the washing that is for the remission of sins, and unto regeneration**, and who is so living as Christ has enjoined"* [*emphasis added*]. [14]

Cardinal Newman also explains that by the time of Constantine the church was thoroughly impregnated with things of pagan origin:

"We are told in various ways by Eusebius, that Constantine, in order to recommend the new religion to the

60

heathen, transferred into it the outward ornaments to which they had been accustomed in their own. It is not necessary to go into a subject which the diligence of Protestant writers has made familiar to most of us. The use of temples, and these dedicated to particular saints, and ornamented on occasions with branches of trees; incense, lamps, and candles; votive offerings on recovery from illness; holy water; asylums; holydays and seasons, use of calendars, processions, blessings on the fields; sacerdotal vestments, the tonsure, the ring in marriage, turning to the East, images at a later date, perhaps the ecclesiastical chant, and the Kyrie Eleison , **are all of pagan origin, and sanctified by their adoption into the Church**" *[emphasis added].* [15]

Cardinal Newman never explains how such practices as baptismal regeneration within the early church were sanctified when they were adopted into the early church. With the condition of the early church in view does it really surprise anyone that these people should expect any favors or that the Lord Jesus would delay His coming to catch up His saints?:

"Look, I am coming soon! My reward is with me, and I will give to each person according to what they have done" (Rev. 22:12).

The Day of the LORD

"Concerning the coming of our Lord Jesus Christ and our being gathered to him, we ask you, brothers and sisters, not to become easily unsettled or alarmed by the teaching allegedly from us--whether by a prophecy or by word of mouth or by letter--asserting that **the day of the Lord** *has already come. Don't let anyone deceive you in any way, for that day will not come until the rebellion occurs and the man of lawlessness is revealed, the man doomed to destruction"* (2 Thess. 2:1-3).

In this passage Paul first speaks of what will happen at the rapture when believers will be gathered to the Lord Jesus. Then we can understand the believers at the church at Thessalonica had received a false report which said that the "day of the LORD" had already come so they wrongly assumed that they missed being raptured, an event which they had been taught would occur before the "day of the LORD." There can be no doubt that the "day of the Lord" is not the same thing as the rapture when believers will put on new, glorious bodies like the body of the Lord Jesus because the "day of the LORD" is described in the following way:

"See, the day of the LORD is coming --a cruel day, with wrath and fierce anger--to make the land desolate and destroy the sinners within it" (Isa. 13:9).

"Woe to you who long for the day of the LORD! Why do you long for the day of the LORD? That day will be darkness, not light" (Amos 5:18).

Woe to those who long for the day of the LORD. On the other hand, putting on new bodies like that of the Lord Jesus is described as the Christian's "hope":

*"Dear friends, now we are children of God, and what we will be has not yet been made known. But we know that when Christ appears, we shall be like him, for we shall see him as he is. All who have **this hope** in him purify themselves, just as he is pure"* (2 Jn. 2-30.

End Notes

1. Gary DeMar, *Last Days Madness*, 37.

2. *The Scofield Study Bible; King James Version*, Note at Matthew 4:17, (New York, NY: Oxford University Press, 2003), 1240.

3. *A Greek English Lexicon*, Liddell & Scott (Oxford: Clarendon Press, 1940), 467.

4. *The Companion Bible, The Authorized Version of 1611* (Grand Rapids: Kregel Publications, 1990), Appendix 6: "Figures of Speech," 12.

5. Joseph Henry Thayer, *A Greek-English Lexicon of the New Testament*, 193.

6. *Vine's Expository Dictionary of New Testament Words*; Accessed December 12, 2018, see "Dictionary Aids" at https://www.blueletterbible.org/lang/lexicon/lexicon.cfm ?strongs=G1551&t=KJV

7. Joseph Henry Thayer, *A Greek-English Lexicon of the New Testament*, 603.

8. *Vine's Complete Expository Dictionary of Old and New Testament Words*, Accesssed December 12, 2018, see"Dictionary Aids" at https://www.blueletterbible.org/lang/lexicon/lexicon.cfm ?Strongs=G603&t=KJV

9. *sermonindex.com*, "Earnest expectation (603) apokaradokia," Accesssed December 4, 2018, http://www.sermonindex.net/modules/articles/index.php? view=article&aid=33937

10. Sir Robert Anderson, *Forgotten Truths* (Grand Rapids: Kregel Publications, 1980), 83-84.

11. Sir Robert Anderson, *Misunderstood Texts of the New Testament* (Grand Rapids: Kregel Publications, 1991), 16-17.

12. Leopold von Ranke, *The Popes of Rome; Sixteenth and Seventeeth Centuries* (London: Blacki And Son, 1846), "Introductory Essay," Merle D'Aubigne'.

13. John Henry Cardinal Newman, *An Essay on the Devolpment of Christian Doctrine* (London: Longmans, Green and Co.,1909), 371-372.

14. Justin Martyr, *First Apology*, Chapter 66; Accessed December 11, 2018, http://www.newadvent.org/fathers/0126.htm

15. John Henry Cardinal Newman, *An Essay on the Devolpment of Christian Doctrine*, 373.

XI. Daniel's Seventy Weeks

Gary DeMar quotes dispensationalist A. J. McClain to stress the importance which dispensationalists place on Daniel's Seventy Weeks: *"For the dispensationalist, 'Probably no single prophetic utterance is more crucial in the fields of Biblical Interpretation, Apologetics, and Eschatology' than the seventy-weeks prophecy of Daniel 9:24-27."* [1]

Even though Gary DeMar thinks that he has the expertise to criticize the interpretation of the Seventy Weeks put forth by dispensationalists he proves that he does not even understand the most basic things in regard to this prophecy. He writes:

*"**Exactly 490 years were to pass for Daniel's people and the Holy City before the Messiah would appear (9: 24)**. Those living in Jesus' day had made the calculations and were expecting 'Messiah the Prince' to appear (9:25)"* [emphasis mine]. [2]

Despite Gary DeMar's assertion that the Messiah would not appear until 490 years the prophecy plainly declares the period "unto Messiah the Prince" is to be 69 weeks of years, and not 70 weeks (490 years):

"Know and understand this: From the time the word goes out to restore and rebuild Jerusalem until the Anointed One, the ruler, comes, there will be seven 'sevens,' and sixty-two 'sevens.' It will be rebuilt with streets and a trench, but in times of trouble" (Dan. 9:25; NIV).

This verse demonstrates that from the commandment to restore Jerusalem until the Messiah will be "seven" sevens and "sixty-two" sevens, a total of sixty nine sevens or exactly 483 years. How can we expect Gary DeMar to have any understanding of this prophecy if he does not even understand the most basic things revealed by the Scriptures?

The First Seven 'Sevens' of Daniel 9:25

In his book *Chronological Aspects of the Life of Christ* Harold Hoehner places the beginning of the prophecy of the Seventy weeks in 444 B.C., writing that *"Nisan 444 B.C. marks the 'terminus a quo' of the seventy weeks of Daniel 9:24-27."* [3]

With the year 444 B.C. in view we can determine that the words "seven 'sevens'" must refer the year 395 B.C.--the same year the Jews received the last revelation from the LORD during Old Testament times, the book of Malachi. Vernon McGee wrote that *"There is some difference of opinion about the time at which Malachi wrote. The date that I suggest is 397 B.C., which is probably a late date."* [4]

The date provided by C.C. Torrey fits McGee's date, writing that *"we may, therefore, assign the book with some confidence to the first half of the fourth century."* [5]

In *The Scofield Study Bible* we read the following about the book of Malachi:

"The final message of the Old Testament contains the prophecy of John the Baptist's ministry, the fulfillment of which begins the New Testament." [6]

Now let us look at Daniel 9:25 again:

*"Know and understand this: '**From the time the word goes out to restore and rebuild Jerusalem until the Anointed One, the ruler, comes, there will be seven 'sevens,' and sixty-two 'sevens.'** It will be rebuilt with streets and a trench, but in times of trouble"* (Dan. 9:25; NIV).

Harold Hoehner says that the 69th 'seven' was fulfilled on the day of The Lord Jesus' triumphal entry into Jerusalem:

"As predicted in Zechhariah 9:9, Christ presented Himself to Israel as Messiah the king the last time and the multitude of the disciples shouted loudly by quoting from a messianic psalm: 'Blessed is the king who comes in the name of the Lord.'" [7]

Daniel 9:26

Let us now look at the words which immediately follow Daniel 9:25:

"After the sixty-two 'sevens,' the Anointed One will be put to death and will have nothing." (Dan.9:26a).

Robert Gundry writes, *"If the cutting off of the Messiah occurred in the middle of the seventieth week, it is very strange that the cutting off is said to be 'after' the sixty-nine weeks (figuring the sum of the seven and the sixty-two weeks). Much more naturally the text would have read 'during' or 'in the midst of' the seventieth week, as it does in verse twenty-seven concerning the stoppage of the sacrifices. The only adequate explanation for this unusual turn of expression is that the seventieth week did not follow on the heels of the sixty-ninth, but that an interval separates the two. The crucifixion then comes shortly 'after' the sixty-ninth but not within the seventieth because of an intervening gap."* [8]

The Gap Between the End of the Sixty-Ninth 'Seven' and the Beginning of the Seventieth 'Seven'

The following verse speaks of the "Seventieth 'Seven'":

*"He will confirm a covenant with many for one 'seven.' In the middle of the 'seven' he will put an end to sacrifice and offering. **And at the temple he will set up an abomination that causes desolation**, until the end that is*

decreed is poured out on him" (Dan. 9:27: NIV).

The person who will make a covenant lasting seven years will also be responsible for the abomination that causes desolation in the Temple, the same exact abomination of which the Lord Jesus spoke of in the following verse:

*"When ye therefore shall see **the abomination of desolation, spoken of by Daniel the prophet, stand in the holy place**...Then let them which be in Judaea flee into the mountains"* (Mt. 24:15-16; KJV).

Hippolytus (170-235 A.D.), an early church father, didn't believe that the abomination of desolation had stood in the holy place in the first century, as witnessed by the fact that he asked, *"and what is the abomination of desolation, but that **when the antichrist comes"** [9]*

These words of the Lord were in answer to his disciples' question concerning what would happen at the "end of the age" (Mt. 24:3). In Chapter II it was pointed out that the end of the age has not yet occurred because at the end of the age there will be a world wide harvest: *"The field is the world"* (Mt. 13:38). Therefore, we can understand that the events described during the first sixty-nine 'sevens' have already occurred but the events described as happening during the seventieth 'seven' remain in the future Therefore, there is indeed a gap of time between the two prophesised time periods.

An Explanation for the "Gap" of Time

In order to explain this "gap" of time Sir Robert Anderson writes that *"when Israel was cast aside the clock of prophetic time was stopped, to be set in motion once again at the close of this intercalary 'Christian dispensation.' And then the Lord's prophetic words shall be fulfilled as though this age of ours had never intervened...But so long as Israel's national position is in abeyance, the stream of fulfillment is tided back; or to change the figure, the hands upon the dial of prophetic time are motionless."* [10]

In regard to the same subject Anderson also wrote the following:

"There exists surely no presumption against supposing that the stream of prophetic time is tided back during all this interval of the apostasy of Judah. The question remains, whether any precedent for this can be discovered in the mystical chronology of Israel's history. According to the book of Kings, Solomon began to build the temple in the 480th year after the children of Israel were come out of the land of Egypt (1 Kings 6:1). This statement, than which none could, seemingly, be more exact, has sorely puzzled chronologers. By some it has been condemned as a forgery, by others it has been dismissed as a blunder; but all have agreed in rejecting it. Moreover, Scripture itself appears to clash with it. In his sermon at Pisidian Antioch (Acts 13:18-21) St. Paul epitomizes thus the chronology of this period of the history of his nation: forty years in the wilderness; 450 years under the judges, and forty years of the reign of Saul; making a total of 530 years. To which must be added the forty years of David's reign and the first three years of Solomon's; making 573 years for the very period which is described in Kings as 480 years. Can these conclusions, apparently so inconsistent, be reconciled? If we follow the history of Israel as detailed in the book of Judges, we shall find that for five several periods their national existence as Jehovah's people was in abeyance. In punishment for their idolatry, God gave them up again and again, and 'sold them into the hands of their enemies.' They became slaves to the king of Mesopotamia for eight years, to the king of Moab for eighteen years, to the king of Canaan for twenty years, to the Midianites for seven years, and finally to the Philistines for forty years. But the sum of 8 +18+ 20+ 7+ 40 years is 93 years, and if 93 years be deducted from 573 years, the result is 480 years. It is obvious, therefore, that the 480 years of the book of Kings from the Exodus to the temple is a mystic era

formed by eliminating every period during which the people were cast off by God. If, then, this principle were intelligible to the Jew in regard to history, it was both natural and legitimate to introduce it in respect of an essentially mystic era like that of the seventy weeks." [11]

"The secret things belong unto the LORD our God" (Deut.29:29).

A study of the OT prophecies demonstrate that the Lord had reasons for not revealing everything that would happen when the Lord Jesus was made flesh and dwelt with men. He kept some things secret. The key to realizing why there is a "gap of time" between the 69th and 70th week is understanding that in the OT prophecies the Lord kept secret the fact that the Jews would reject their promised Messiah at His first advent. The OT prophecies were written in such a way that would give the nation no excuse for rejecting and crucifying the Lord Jesus.

According to prophecy Israel was to be the LORD's agent for bringing all the nations to the light of the gospel (Isa. 61:8, 55:3-5, Zech. 8:8, 13, 23). But since that nation rejected their promised Messiah, which was a secret or "mystery" not revealed in the OT, the promises to Israel in regard to the 70th Week have been postponed until the "until the full number of the Gentiles has come in":

"I do not want you to be ignorant of this mystery, brothers and sisters, so that you may not be conceited: Israel has experienced a hardening in part until the full number of the Gentiles has come in, and in this way all Israel will be saved. As it is written: 'The deliverer will come from Zion; he will turn godlessness away from Jacob' (Ro. 11:25-26).

So the "gap" between the 69th and 70th week was not revealed in the OT prophecies. It was kept secret. And the fulfillment of the 70th week awaits the time when the "*the*

70

full number of the Gentiles has come in."

End Notes

1. Gary DeMar, *Last Days Madness*, 329.

2. *Ibid.,* 343.

3. Harold W. Hoehner, *Chronological Aspects of the Life of Christ* (Grand Rapids: Zondervan Publishing House, 1975), 128.

4. J. Vernon McGee, *Thru the Bible Commentary* (Nashville, TN: Thomas Nelson Publishers, 1991), "Malachi" Volume 33.

5. C.C. Torrey, "The Prophecy of Malachi," *Journal of Biblical Literature,* (Seventeenth Year, 1898), 14.

6. *The Scofield Study Bible; King James Version*, "The Book of Malachi; Background," 1219.

7. Harold W. Hoehner, *Chronological Aspects of the Life of Christ*, 139.

8. Robert H. Gundry, *The Church and the Tribulation* (Grand Rapids: Zondervan Publishing House, 1973), 190.

9. *A Dictionary of Early Christian Beliefs* ed. David W. Borcott [Peabody, MA: Hendrickson Publishing Marketing LLC, 2013], 188.

10. Sir Robert Anderson, *Forgotten Truths*, 72-73.

11. Sir Robert Anderson, *The Coming Prince* (Grand Rapids: Kregel Classics, 1957), 81-84.

XII. Daniel's Seventy Weeks; Part 2

Church History

Gary DeMar attempts to prove that there is no reason to believe that there is a "gap of time" or "parenthesis" between the end of the 69th week and the beginning of the 70th week by appealing to "church history":

"Why is there no mention of this 'great parenthesis' either in the Bible or in the nearly nineteen hundred years of church history?" [1]

The earliest commentary on the Seventy Weeks of Daniel was written by Hippolytus, and according to his view the 70th week did not follow immediately after the end of the 69th week. He believed that the fulfillment of the 70th Week remained in the future and therefore a "gap of time" is a necessity to support his view:

*"For when the sixty-two weeks are fulfilled, and Christ has come, and the gospel is preached in every place, the times will be accomplished. Then, there will remain only one week (the last), in which Elijah and Enoch will appear. And in the middle of it, the abomination of desolation will be manifested. This is the Antichrist, announcing desolation to the world. **And when he comes**, the sacrifices and oblation will be removed, which are now offered to God in every place by the nations"* [emphasis added]. [2]

Fulfillment of the Seventieth Week

After the children of Israel are saved then we read of the

blessings which will descend upon David's people (the children of Israel) and upon his city (Jerusalem):

"Seventy 'sevens' are decreed for your people and your holy city to finish transgression, to put an end to sin, to atone for wickedness, to bring in everlasting righteousness, to seal up vision and prophecy and to anoint the Most Holy Place" (Dan. 9:24).

1) *"to finish the transgression "* Let us look at the following translation:

*"Seventy weeks have been determined concerning your people and your holy city **to put an end to rebellion**"* (Dan. 9:24; NET).

That will begin during the "great tribulation" when the "rebels" and those who "transgress against" the LORD will be purged:

*"I will take note of you as you pass under my rod, and I will bring you into the bond of the covenant. **I will purge you of those who revolt and rebel against me**"* (Ez. 20:37-38).

This is also called the *"a time of trouble for Jacob"* : *" 'How awful that day will be! No other will be like it. It will be a time of trouble for Jacob, but he will be saved out of it. 'In that day,' declares the LORD Almighty, 'I will break the yoke off their necks and will tear off their bonds; no longer will foreigners enslave them' "* (Jer. 30:7-8).

2) *"to put an end to sin"* The word "sin" basically means "lawlessness":

*"Everyone who sins breaks the law; in fact, **sin is lawlessness**"* (1 Jn. 3:4).

The "end of sins" in regard to Israel will happen when the nation receives the *"spirit of grace"*:

"On that day I will set out to destroy all the nations that attack Jerusalem. And I will pour out on the house of David and the inhabitants of Jerusalem a spirit of grace and supplication. They will look on me, the one they have

pierced, and they will mourn for him as one mourns for an only child, and grieve bitterly for him as one grieves for a firstborn son (Zech. 12:9-10).

"For I will take you out of the nations; I will gather you from all the countries and bring you back into your own land...And I will put my Spirit in you and move you to follow my decrees and be careful to keep my laws" (Ez. 36:24,27).

3) *"to atone for wickedness."* In this sense the word "atone"means to cleanse from sins, as witnessed by the following verse which speaks of the "day of atonement":

"...on this day atonement will be made for you, to cleanse you. Then, before the LORD, you will be clean from all your sins" (Lev. 16:30).

We can see this will happen "in that day", the time when the Lord Jesus will return to save Israel from her enemies:

*"On that day a fountain will be opened to the house of David and the inhabitants of Jerusalem, **to cleanse them from sin and impurity***" (Zech. 13:1).

4) *"and to bring in everlasting righteousness ."* This is in regard to the fact that the Lord Jesus will be in the midst of Israel "forever":

"They will live in the land I gave to my servant Jacob, the land where your ancestors lived. They and their children and their children's children will live there forever" (Ez. 37:25).

Only in this way will the nation of Israel enjoy "everlasting righteousness": *"Your righteousness is everlasting and your law is true"* (Ps. 119:142).

5) *"to seal up vision and prophecy"* The word translated "seal up" carries the idea of "completion". Harry Bultema writes: *"A scroll was not complete until it was completely filled. Thus this sealing of a scroll became a symbol of fulfillment (Isa. 8:16)."* [3]

At the end of the 70th week the vision and prophecy of Daniel concerning the Seventy weeks will be complete.

6) *"and to anoint the most Holy."* Albert Barnes wrote that the words "the most holy" *"properly means 'holy of holies'...It is applied often in the Scriptures to the 'inner sanctuary,' or the portion of the tabernacle and temple containing the ark of the covenant, the two tables of stone."* [4]

Leon Wood writes that *"The phrase "holy of holies" (qodesh qadash'm) occurs, either with or without the article, thirty-nine times in the Old Testament, **always in reference to the Tabernacle or Temple or to the holy articles used in them**. When referring to the most holy place, where the Ark was kept, the article is regularly used (e.g., Ex. 26: 33), but it is not when referring to the holy articles (e.g., Ex. 29: 37) or to the whole Temple complex (e.g., Ezek. 43: 12). **In view of these matters, it is highly likely that the phrase refers to the Temple also here, which, in view of the context, must be a future Temple**; and, since the phrase is used without the article, reference must be to a complex of that Temple, rather than its most holy place"* [emphasis mine]. [5]

Gary DeMar writes, *"There is nothing in Daniel 9:24-27 that even hints that there will be a rebuilt temple"* [6]

Again, the following words of the Lord Jesus were in answer to what will happen at the "end of the age" (Mt. 24:3) and He spoke of "the holy place" of which Daniel wrote and which is associated with the temple:

*"So when you see standing in **the holy place** 'the abomination that causes desolation,' **spoken of through the prophet Daniel**--let the reader understand--then let those who are in Judea flee to the mountains"* (Mt. 24:15-16; NIV).

Earlier the Lord Jesus spoke the parable of the "tares of the field" where He described what would occur at the "end of the age":

*"He that soweth the good seed is the Son of man; **The field is the world**; the good seed are the children of the kingdom; but the tares are the children of the wicked one; The enemy that sowed them is the devil; **the harvest is the***

end of the age; and the reapers are the angels. As therefore the tares are gathered and burned in the fire; so shall it be in the end of this age.. The Son of man shall send forth his angels, and they shall gather out of his kingdom all things that offend, and them which do iniquity; And shall cast them into a furnace of fire: there shall be wailing and gnashing of teeth. Then shall the righteous shine forth as the sun in the kingdom of their Father. Who hath ears to hear, let him hear" (Mt. 13:37-43).

Here we can see that the Lord Jesus speaks of a harvest that will happen at the "end of the age", the "end of this age." He also makes it clear that the harvest will take place in the field, and He says that the *"field is the world."*

Since there has never been a world-wide harvest then common sense dictates that the "end of the age" has not yet happened so the events described by the Lord Jesus at Matthew 24:15-16 remain in the future and the Lord Jesus does speak of "the holy place" which refers to a rebuilt temple.

End Notes

1. Gary DeMar, *Last Days Madness*, 95.

2. *A Dictionary of Early Christian Beliefs,* ed. David W. Borcot, 188.

3. Harry Bultema, *Commentary on Daniel* (Grand Rapids: Kregel, 1988), 283.

4. Albert Barnes, *Notes on the Bible* (1834), Commentary at Daniel 9:24; Accessed December 213, 2018, https://biblehub.com/commentaries/barnes/daniel/9.htm

5. Leon Wood, *A Commentary on Daniel* (Grand Rapids: Zondervan, 1973), 250.

6. Gary DeMar, *Last Days Madness*, 95

XIII. This Generation

In the "Introduction" to *Last Days Madness* Gary DeMar states that his first dissatisfaction with the futurist system came because of Matthew 24:34:

"The first area of dissatisfaction came with how commentators handled Matthew 24:34: **'Truly I say to you, this generation will not pass away until all these things take place**.' *At first reading one gets the distinct impression that Jesus is saying that the people with whom He was speaking would live to see and experience the events described in Matthew 24. This seemed impossible! And yet, there it was...If this is the correct interpretation, as I believe it is and hope to prove in the course of this book, then today's speculative madness relating to repeated failed attempts at predicting the end must be attributed to a gross misunderstanding of Bible prophecy"* [*emphasis mine*]. [1]

Although the mistaken idea that the Greek words translated "this generation" must refer to the generation living at the time the Lord Jesus walked the earth is but one link in a multitude of errors promoted by the preterists, it is the first and most important. As already demonstrated, the generation living when the Lord spoke the words at Matthew 24:34 never saw a world wide harvest:

"There will be signs in the sun, moon and stars. On the earth, nations will be in anguish and perplexity at the roaring and tossing of the sea. **People will faint from terror, apprehensive of what is coming on the world**, *for the heavenly bodies will be shaken. At that time they will see the Son of Man coming in a cloud with power and great glory...Be careful, or your hearts will be weighed down with carousing, drunkenness and the anxieties of life, and that day will close on you suddenly like a trap.* **For it will come on all**

those who live on the face of the whole earth" (Lk. 21:25-27, 34-35).

Gary DeMar writes, *"I believe the Bible. There is no way that it could err. This was my starting presupposition. Scripture had to be taken at face value."* [2]

If Gary DeMar takes the Scriptures at face value then why does he continue to deny that the words penned by Luke in the twenty-first chapter of his gospel are speaking of a world wide judgment? Why does he continue to deny that the judgment at the "end of the age" is in regard to the whole earth?:

" *He answered, 'The one who sowed the good seed is the Son of Man.* **The field is the world**, *and the good seed stands for the people of the kingdom. The weeds are the people of the evil one, and the enemy who sows them is the devil.* **The harvest is the end of the age**...*The Son of Man will send out his angels, and they will weed out of his kingdom everything that causes sin and all who do evil. They will throw them into the blazing furnace, where there will be weeping and gnashing of teeth*" (Mt. 13:37-39, 41-42).

The Correct Meaning of *Genea* in the Olivet Discourse

The Greek word translated "generation" is *genea* and Joseph Henry Thayer gives one of the defintions of the word as follows: "*that which has been begotten,* **men of the same stock, a family**...*the several ranks of natural descent, the successive members of a genealogy*" [emphasis added]. [3]

Vine's Expository Dictionary of New Testament Words gives the following as one of the meanings of the word:

"*connected with 'ginomai,' 'to become,' primarily signifies 'a begetting, or birth;' hence, that which has been begotten,* **a family; or successive members of a genealogy**, *Mat 1:17,* **or of a race of people**, *possessed of similar* *characteristics, pursuits, etc., (of a bad character) Mat 17:17; Mar 9:19; Luk 9:41; 16:8; Act 2:40"* [*emphasis added*]. [4]

We also see one of the meanings which match the previous two on *The Online Liddell-Scott-Jones Greek-English Lexicon*:

*"1. race, **family**...tribe, **nation**"* [*emphasis added*]. [5]

Here we see that the word *genea* can mean "nation" and it is translated that way in the following verse:

*"That ye may be blameless and harmless, the sons of God, without rebuke, in the midst of a crooked and perverse **nation (genea)**, among whom ye shine as lights in the world"* (Phil. 2:15; KJV).

We also know that the family of Abraham, Isaac and Jacob was made a nation while in Egypt:

*" 'I am God, the God of your father,' he said. 'Do not be afraid to go down to Egypt, **for I will make you into a great nation there** "* (Gen. 46:3).

Therefore, there can be no doubt that one of the meanings of the Greek word *genea* is "family, " or, in this case, a "nation." Now it will be demonstrated that is the correct translation of Matt. 24:34.

This *Genea* Shall Not Pass

By the Lord Jesus' own admission the "times" and "seasons" have been put in the Father's power (Acts 1:7). He said that only the Father knew the time when His Olivet prophecy would be fulfilled:

*"But about that day or hour no one knows, not even the angels in heaven, **nor the Son, but only the Father**"* (Mt. 24:36).

Evidently He had no foreknowledge in regard to the time

when all these things would be fulfilled. Instead, He was the Prophet described here:

*"I will raise up for them a prophet like you from among their fellow Israelites, **and I will put my words in his mouth. He will tell them everything I command him**"* (Deut. 18:18).

The Lord Jesus had no special knowledge in regard to when the things would happen so He certainly would not be pointing out any specific generation of men who would see the signs of which He spoke.

Therefore there is nothing in the Bible which indicates that the Lord Jesus would know that His prophecies would be fulfilled during the time of any specific generation. After all, in order for the Lord Jesus to be sent back to earth the Jewish nation was required to "repent," as witnessed by the following words of Peter on the day of Pentecost:

*"**Repent, then, and turn to God**, so that your sins may be wiped out, that times of refreshing may come from the Lord, **and that he may send the Messiah, who has been appointed for you**--even Jesus"* (Acts 3:19-20).

Since the nation of Israel did not repent and turn to the Lord it is obvious that the Lord Jesus was not sent back to earth. Therefore the generation then living did not see all of the signs:

*"And then shall appear the sign of the Son of man in heaven: and then shall all the tribes of the earth mourn, and **they shall see the Son of man coming in the clouds of heaven** with power and great glory...So likewise ye, **when ye shall see all these things**, know that it is near, even at the doors. Verily I say unto you, This generation shall not pass, till all these things be fuffilled"* (Mt. 24:30, 33-34).

Therefore, the correct translation of the following passage is as follows:

*"Even so, when you see all these things, you know that it is near, right at the door. Truly I tell you, this **nation** will certainly not pass away until all these things have happened"*

(Mt. 24:33-34).

Again, the the nation is made up of the physical descendants or family of Abraham, Isaac and Jacob.

The Lord Jesus' sermon foretold of the "great tribulation," a time when Israel will be attacked unmercifully in an attempt to destroy the whole family of Abraham, Isaac and Jacob. Therefore it would not be unusual for the Lord Jesus to assure them that they will not be wiped out and that they will continue to exist. Therefore, He told them that the family of Abraham, Isaac and Jacob would still be in existence when He returned to the earth.

In fact, this is not the first time that such assurance had been given to the Israelites, as witnessed by these words:

"Thus says the LORD, Who gives the sun for light by day And the fixed order of the moon and the stars for light by night, Who stirs up the sea so that its waves roar; The LORD of hosts is His name: **If this fixed order departs From before Me, declares the LORD, Then the offspring of Israel also will cease from being a nation** *before Me forever"* (Jer. 31:35-36).

According to the Lord as long as the sun and moon remain in the sky the nation of Israel will remain "being a nation" before Him. So there is nothing odd about the Lord Jesus telling the Israelites that "this nation shall not pass till all these things be fulfilled," especially with the great tribulation in view.

When "You" Shall See All These Things

Now let us look at the following passage with the correct translation:

"Even so, when **you** *see all these things,* **you** *know that it is near, right at the door. Truly I tell you, this nation will certainly not pass away until all these things have happened"*

(Mt. 24:33-34).

At another place the Lord Jesus used the pronouns "you" and "ye" in regard to those who were not members of the then present generation but instead will belong to a future generation:

" *O Jerusalem, Jerusalem, which killest the prophets, and stonest them that are sent unto thee; how often would I have gathered thy children together, as a hen doth gather her brood under her wings, and ye would not! Behold, your house is left unto you desolate:* **and verily I say unto you, Ye shall not see me, until the time come when ye shall say, Blessed is he that cometh in the name of the Lord**" (Lk. 34:35; KJV).

Earlier His disciples had indeed said,"*Blessed is he who comes in the name of the Lord!*" (Mt.21:9) so if we are to believe the words of the Lord Jesus then at some time in the future there will be some Jews who will say those words. And the Lord used the pronoun "you" to refer to those who will belong to a future generation.

With that fact established we can understand that the word "you" in the following verse can refer to Jews belonging to a future generation. Therefore the prounoun can be in reference to not only the Israelites living in the then present generation but also to all of Israelites throughout time:

"*Even so, when* **you** *see all these things,* **you** *know that it is near, right at the door. Truly I tell you, this nation will certainly not pass away until all these things have happened*" (Mt. 24:33-34).

End Notes

1. Gary DeMar, *Last Days Madness*, 14-15.

2. *Ibid.*, 14.

3. Joseph Henry Thayer, *A Greek English Lexicon of the New Testament*, 112.

4. *Vine's Expository Dictionary of New Testament Words*; Accessed December 13, 2018, https://www.blueletterbible.org/lang/lexicon/lexicon.cfm?Strongs=G1074&t=KJV; see "Dictionary Aids": *Vine's Expository Dictionary.*

5. *LSJ: The Online Liddell-Scott-Jones Greek-English Lexicon*, Accessed December 13, 2018, http://stephanus.tlg.uci.edu/lsj/#eid=22531&context=lsj&action=from-search

XIV. *"Shall Not Taste Death"*– Matthew 16:27-28

" 'For the Son of Man is going to come in his Father's glory with his angels, and then he will reward each person according to what they have done. Truly I tell you, some who are standing here will not taste death before they see the Son of Man coming in his kingdom' (Mt.16:27-28)

In regard to this verse Gary DeMar asks,"*If we maintain that the event Jesus is describing is still in our future, then how do we interpret His statement that some of those with whom He was speaking would still be alive when He did in fact 'come in the glory of His Father with His angels' ?"* [1]

In order to correctly understand what the Lord Jesus said in this passage we must undertand that one of the meanings of the Greek word translated "coming" in verse 28 is "*to appear, make one's appearance.*" [2]

Therefore, the correct translation of the verse is as follows:

"*Truly I tell you, some who are standing here will not taste death before they see the Son of Man **appearing** in his kingdom.*"

From this we can understand that the Lord Jesus was saying that there were some of the Apostles who would see the Lord Jesus "appearing" in His kingdom before they died. The following words of Peter refer to this "appearing," and it happened at the "transfiguration" on the holy mount:

"*For, skilfully devised fables not having followed out, we did make known to you the power and **presence of our Lord Jesus Christ**, but eye-witnesses having become of **his majesty** --for having received from God the Father honour and glory,*

86

such a voice being borne to him by the excellent glory: 'This is My Son -- the beloved, in whom I was well pleased;' and this voice we -- we did hear, out of heaven borne, being with him in the holy mount" (2 Pet.1:16-18; YLT).

Peter is speaking of seeing the Lord's "presence" and His "majesty" and the following passage follows immediately after the Lord Jesus said that there were some who were with Him who would not taste death until they see Him appearing in his kingdom:

"*After six days Jesus took with him Peter, James and John the brother of James, and led them up a high mountain by themselves. **There he was transfigured before them. His face shone like the sun, and his clothes became as white as the light**" (Mt.17:1-2).

In each gospel that records the words of the Lord Jesus saying that some of His Apostles will see Him in the kingdom the events of the "transfiguration" immediately follow.

Louis A. Barbieri, Jr., writes the following concerning the significance of those who were present on the Holy Mount:

"*Why were Moses and Elijah, of all Old Testament people, present on this occasion? Perhaps these two men and the disciples suggest all the categories of people who will be in Jesus' coming kingdom. The disciples represent individuals who will be present in physical bodies. Moses represents saved individuals who have died or will die. Elijah represents saved individuals who will not experience death, but will be caught up to heaven alive (1 Thes. 4:17). These three groups will be present when Christ institutes His kingdom on earth. Furthermore, the Lord will be in His glory as He was at the transfiguration, and the kingdom will take place on earth, as this obviously did.*" [3]

Objections

Gary DeMar says, *"Some claim that the 'coming' Jesus had in mind was the transfiguration. But the transfiguration cannot be its fulfillment since Jesus indicated that some who were standing with Him would still be alive when He came but most would be dead."* [4]

The Lord Jesus never said that most of His Apostles would be dead by the time when some of them saw Him coming in His kingdom. He was merely saying that some of them would be given the privilege of seeing Him in His kingdom before they died. If we look at the context we can see that it was here that the Lord told His Apostles that He would suffer and die (16:21). Not only that He also told them to follow Him and that whoever shall lose his life for His sake shall find it (16:25).

Surely this would raise questions in the minds of His Apostles. If the Lord was to die what would that mean about the kingdom? Would the prophecies of the OT in regard to the kingdom be fulfilled? His Apostles would need reassurance at this point in time that He would ultimately triumph and the kingdom would indeed be set up. In order to reassure them He told them that some of them would see Him appearing in His kingdom before they died. So by understanding the context in which His words were spoken we can know that He was not saying that most of His Apostles would die before some of them saw Him appearing in His kingdom.

John 16: 27-28

Gary DeMar next attempts to use John 21:18-23 to prove that the coming of the Lord Jesus has already happened and some of His Apostles were still alive at that coming:

"A helpful bibical commentary on Matthew 16:27-28 is found in John 21:18-23. After Jesus describes for Peter how he will die (21:18), Peter asks of John's fate, 'Lord, and what about this man?' (21:21). Jesus says to Peter, 'If I want him to remain until I come, what is that to you? You follow Me!' (21:22). History tells us that Peter died before Jerusalem was destroyed, and John lived beyond Jerusalem's destruction, a perfect and expected fulfillment of Matthew 16:27-28." [5]

If we are to believe Gary DeMar then we must believe that the Lord Jesus prophesised that John would not die before the Lord Jesus came in glory. However, the verses which follow prove that Gary DeMar made the same mistake that the Apostles made when they assumed that is what the Lord Jesus said. Let us look at the verse which Gary DeMar left out:

"When Peter saw him, he asked, 'Lord, what about him?' Jesus answered, 'If I want him to remain alive until I return, what is that to you? You must follow me.' Because of this, the rumor spread among the believers that this disciple would not die. But Jesus did not say that he would not die; he only said, 'If I want him to remain alive until I return, what is that to you?'" (Jn. 21:21-23; NIV).

At least one of the Apostles went about telling other believers that John would not die until the Lord Jesus came. And that is what Mr. DeMar is asserting that the Lord Jesus said. But John himself says, *"But Jesus did not say that he would not die"*

Instead the Lord Jesus said, *"If I want him to remain alive until I return, what is that to you?"*

Edwin A. Blum says, *"Peter, having been informed about God's plan for his life, naturally wondered what the future held for his friend John, the disciple whom Jesus loved. Jesus sharply rebuked Peter for being curious about God's will for another's life: What is that to you? You must follow Me. Some disciples can be easily distracted by unnecessary questions about God's secret will; as a result they neglect God's plainly revealed will...Peter was to commit himself to God's plain commands to him. John then corrected a faulty inference made by some believers that John would not die."* [6]

Even with these plain words before him Gary DeMar makes a faulty inference in regard to what the Lord Jesus actually said. He should take his own advice when he wrote, *"Why is a discussion of these texts so important? First, we want to be accurate in our understanding of Scripture since it is God's only word to us, the expression of His will. To misinterpret Scripture is to misinterpret God's will. Second, the integrity of the Bible is at stake."* [7]

Gary DeMar did in fact misinterpret the Scriptures and thus he misinterpreted God's will.

Did the High Priest See the Coming of the Lord Jesus?

The Preterists invaribly quote the following passage in their attempt to prove that the high priest saw the Lord Jesus come to the earth in the first century to destroy Jerusalem:

*"The high priest said to him, 'I charge you under oath by the living God: Tell us if you are the Messiah, the Son of God.' 'You have said so,' Jesus replied. 'But I say to all of you: From now on you will **see (horao)** the Son of Man sitting at the right hand of the Mighty One and coming on the clouds of heaven"* (Mt. 26:63-64).

In the NASB Lexicon [8] the word Greek word translated as "see" is *horah*, the Greek word with the Numerical Code of # 3708. One of the meanings of that word is *"to see with the mind, to perceive, know"* [9]

In *HELPS Word Study* one of the meanings given is: *"properly, see, often with metaphorical meaning: 'to see with the mind' (i.e. spiritually see), i.e. perceive (with inward spiritual perception)"* [10]

90

From this we can conclude that the Lord Jesus told the high priest that in some time in the future he preceive or see with his mind that the Lord Jesus is at the right hand of God and will also know of His coming to the earth in glory to usher in the earthly kingdom. However, the high priest will no longer be alive when that happens.

End Notes

1. Gary DeMar, *Last Days Madness*, 43.

2. Joseph Henry Thayer, *A Greek-English Lexicon of the New Testament*, 251.

3. Louis A. Barbieri, Jr., "Matthew"; *The Bible Knowledge Commentary; New Testament* ed. John F. Walvoord and Roy B. Zuck (Colorado Springs: ChariotVictor Press, 1983), 59.

4. Gary DeMar, *Last Days Madness*, 43-44.

5. *Ibid.*, 44.

6. Edwin A. Blum, "John"; *The Bible Knowledge Commentary; New Testament*, 345-346.

7. Gary DeMar, *Last Days Madness*, 46.

8. *NASB Lexicon* of Matthew 26:64; Accessed December 21, 2018, https://biblehub.com/lexicon/matthew/26-64.htm

9. Joseph Henry Thayer, *A Greek-English Lexicon of the New Testament*, 451.

10. *HELPS Word Studies*; Accessed December 21, 2018, https://biblehub.com/greek/3708.htm

XV. You Will Not Finish Going Through the Towns of Israel

The Preterists often quote the following verse to try to prove that the Lord Jesus has already "come" in one form or another to the earth:

"When you are persecuted in one place, flee to another. Truly I tell you, you will not finish going through the towns of Israel before the Son of Man comes" (Mt. 10:23).

In his comments on the "context" where this verse is found Gary DeMar writes:

"Who is Jesus addressing in Matthew 10:23? The immediate context tells us: 'Behold, I send you out as sheep in the midst of wolves; therefore be shrewd as serpents and innocent as doves' (Matt. 10:16). Throughout His discourse, Jesus has His present audience in mind. Like in Matthew 24, Jesus uses the second person plural ('you') throughout the passage to make this point more than clear. There is nothing in these chapters that gives any indication that Jesus has any other audience in view other than His immediate audience" [1]

Even though the Lord used the word "you" when speaking to the Jews then present that word can refer to those who will live in a future generation. Again, let us look at the following words of the Lord Jesus spoken to the Jews:

*"O Jerusalem, Jerusalem, which killest the prophets, and stonest them that are sent unto thee; how often would I have gathered thy children together, as a hen doth gather her brood under her wings, and ye would not! Behold, your house is left unto you desolate: and verily **I say unto you, Ye shall not see me, until the time come when ye shall say, Blessed is he that cometh in the name of the Lord**"* (Lk. 34:35; KJV).

Earlier His disciples had indeed said,"*Blessed is he who comes in the name of the Lord!*" (Mt.21:9) so if we are to believe the words of the Lord Jesus then at some time in the future there will be some Jews who will say those words. And the Lord used the pronoun "you" to refer to those who will belong to a future generation.

Next, we will see that the seven verses which precede Matthew 10:23 are speaking about the same exact events foretold by the Lord Jesus at Mark 19:9-13 and what we will read there will prove that the word "you" found at Matthew 10:16 must refer to a future generation of Jews. First, let's compare the verse in question from the book of Matthew with those found in the gospel of Mark, beginning with Matthew:

"*I am sending you out like sheep among wolves. Therefore be as shrewd as snakes and as innocent as doves. Be on your guard; you will be handed over to the local councils and be flogged in the synagogues. On my account you will be brought before governors and kings as witnesses to them and to the Gentiles*" (Mt. 13:16-18).

Now we see verses from the gospel of Mark which speak of these same exact events:

"*You must be on your guard. You will be handed over to the local councils and flogged in the synagogues. On account of me you will stand before governors and kings as witnesses to them*" (Mk. 13:9)

Now let us continue from the Lord's narrative from the gospel of Matthew:

"*But when they arrest you, do not worry about what to say or how to say it. At that time you will be given what to say, for it will not be you speaking, but the Spirit of your Father speaking through you. Brother will betray brother to death, and a father his child; children will rebel against their parents and have them put to death. You will be hated by everyone because of me, but the one who stands firm to the end will be saved*" (Mt. 10:19-21).

That matches perfectly with what we read in the gospel of Mark:

"Whenever you are arrested and brought to trial, do not worry beforehand about what to say. Just say whatever is given you at the time, for it is not you speaking, but the Holy Spirit. Brother will betray brother to death, and a father his child. Children will rebel against their parents and have them put to death. Everyone will hate you because of me, but the one who stands firm to the end will be saved" (Mk. 13:11-13).

The very next verse from the gospel of Mark proves beyond any doubt that the word "you" must refer to a future generation of Jews because it has already been proven that only a future generation of Jews will see the abomination of desolation stand in the holy place:

*"When **you** see '**the abomination that causes desolation'standing where it does not belong**--let the reader understand--then let those who are in Judea flee to the mountains"* (Mk. 13:14).

Again, the Lord Jesus' words in regard to those seeing the abomination stand in the holy place in the gospel of Matthew (Mt. 24:15) were in answer to what would happen at the end of the age:

*"As Jesus was sitting on the Mount of Olives, the disciples came to him privately. 'Tell us,' they said, 'when will this happen, and what will be the sign of your coming and of **the end of the age?**'"* (Mt. 24:3).

Earlier the Lord spoke of what exactly will happen at the "end of the age" and common sense dictates that the events He said will come to pass at the "end of the age" have not yet happened:

*"Then he left the crowd and went into the house. His disciples came to him and said, 'Explain to us the parable of the weeds in the field.' He answered, 'The one who sowed the good seed is the Son of Man. **The field is the world**, and the*

*good seed stands for the people of the kingdom. The weeds are the people of the evil one, and the enemy who sows them is the devil. **The harvest is the end of the age**, and the harvesters are angels. As the weeds are pulled up and burned in the fire, **so it will be at the end of the age**. The Son of Man will send out his angels, **and they will weed out of his kingdom everything that causes sin and all who do evil.** They will throw them into the blazing furnace, where there will be weeping and gnashing of teeth. Then the righteous will shine like the sun in the kingdom of their Father"* (Mt. 13:36-43).

There has never been a world-wide harvest at anytime in the past so the events which will happen at the "end of the age" remain in the future, including the one described by the Lord Jesus in the following verse:

"When you are persecuted in one place, flee to another. Truly I tell you, you will not finish going through the towns of Israel before the Son of Man comes" (Mt. 10:23).

The Preterists have not learned to integrate the different accounts of the events which will happen in the future spoken by the Lord Jesus in His Olivet discourse so they remain confused in regard to what the Lord was actually teaching in that discourse. In the next chapter we will once again see that Gary DeMar, while claiming to be an expert on the Olivet discourse, remains blind to what the Lord Jesus was actually teaching.

End Notes

1. Gary DeMar, "Context! Context! Context!" *The Americal Vision*, Accessed December 18, 2018, https://americanvision.org/4806/context-context-context/

XVI. The Destruction of the Temple in the First Century

Gary DeMar writes that "*The disciples clearly equated the desctruction of the temple with Jesus' 'coming' in judgment, which would result in the end of the age.*" [1]

In the Olivet discourse recorded by Luke we see the disciples asking the Lord questions about the temple and their questions were strictly limited to the temple then standing:

"*Some of his disciples were remarking about how the temple was adorned with beautiful stones and with gifts dedicated to God. But Jesus said, 'As for what you see here, the time will come when not one stone will be left on another; every one of them will be thrown down.' 'Teacher,' they asked, 'when will these things happen? And what will be the sign that they are about to take place?'*" (Lk. 21:5-7).

Please notice that the question has nothing at all to do with the coming of the Lord Jesus or the end of the age but instead was limited to the time and signs leading up to the destruction of the temple then standing. The first thing of interest we should notice is the fact that when the Lord Jesus was specifically asked about His coming and the end of the age (Mt.24:3) He said that seeing the abomination of desolation standing in the holy place was the time when the Jews should flee to the mountains:

"*So when you see standing in the holy place 'the abomination that causes desolation,' spoken of through the prophet Daniel--let the reader understand--then let those who are in Judea flee to the mountains*" (Mt. 24:15-16).

On the other hand, in the book of Luke the Lord makes no mention at all of the abomination of desolation and says that the people are to flee to the mountains at the time when they see Jerusalem surrounded by armies and not at the time when they will see the abomination of desolation stand in the holy place:

"When you see Jerusalem being surrounded by armies, you will know that its desolation is near. Then let those who are in Judea flee to the mountains, let those in the city get out, and let those in the country not enter the city" (Lk. 21:20-21).

This alone provides proof that the event when the temple was destroyed in the first century is an entirely different event than the great tribulation. Besides that, what we see in Luke's account is a complete and total victory for the armies who came against Jerusalem--*"They will fall by the sword and will be taken as prisoners to all the nations"* (Lk. 21:24). These things were fulfilled in 70 AD.

On the other hand, when the Lord was asked about the sign of His coming and the end of the age He spoke about the time of the great tribulation being shortened and in Chapter IX we saw that it was the Lord's return at the end of the great tribulation which resulted in the time being shortened because then he will fight against all the nations which will come against Jerusalem (Zech.14:3). So in Luke's account we see Jerusalem totally defeated while in Matthew the time of the great tribulation will be shortened and we know it will be shortened when the Lord Jesus returns to the earth and wages war against the nations who will come against Jerusalem. And that is exactly what the Lord Jesus is speaking about in Luke's account:

*"They will fall by the sword and will be taken as prisoners to all the nations. **Jerusalem will be trampled on by the Gentiles until the times of the Gentiles are fulfilled**"* (Lk. 21:24).

In his commentary on this verse John A. Martin writes the following:

"Jerusalem will again fall under Gentile domination in

the Tribulation (Zech. 14:1-2) just before the Messiah returns to restore Jerusalem" [2]

That explains the words of the Lord Jesus in the next verse because the events of which He speaks there will follow after the Lord Jesus restores Jerusalem and from then on will no longer be trampled on by the Gentiles:

"There will be signs in the sun, moon and stars. On the earth, nations will be in anguish and perplexity at the roaring and tossing of the sea. People will faint from terror, apprehensive of what is coming on the world, for the heavenly bodies will be shaken. At that time they will see the Son of Man coming in a cloud with power and great glory" (Lk. 21:25-27)

By the time the signs will be seen in the sky the great tribulation will be over (Mt.24:29) and after the signs are seen in the sky the Lord Jesus will leave Jerusalem and be seen in the rest of the world:

"The sun and moon will be darkened, and the stars no longer shine. The LORD will roar from Zion and thunder from Jerusalem; the earth and the heavens will tremble" (Joel 3:15-16).

Here we read that the earth and the heavens will tremble and that is exactly what will happen because the Lord Jesus said that *"People will faint from terror, apprehensive of what is coming on the world, for the heavenly bodies will be shaken"* (Lk. 21:26).

When we look at the verses which follow in the gospel of Luke we can understand that the Lord Jesus' coming in a cloud means that the Jew's redemption is near and the "redemption" refers to the kingdom which the Lord Jesus also says is near:

"At that time they will see the Son of Man coming in a cloud with power and great glory. When these things begin to take place, stand up and lift up your heads, because your redemption is drawing near (eggizo).' He told them this

parable: 'Look at the fig tree and all the trees. When they sprout leaves, you can see for yourselves and know that summer is near. Even so, when you see these things happening, you know that **the kingdom of God is near (eggizo)** *'* " (Lk. 21:28-31).

So when we examine the Olivet discourse as presented in the gospel of Luke we see that the disciples only asked the Lord Jesus about what was going to happen to the temple then standing and nothing more. And the answer the Lord Jesus gave provided evidence that the circumstances surrounding the destruction of the temple then standing in the first century were different from the circumstances of which He spoke concerning the great tribulation. Then after speaking about the temple the Lord went beyond answering the disciple's original question and expanded His remarks to include His coming to set up His earthly kingdom.

Despite these facts Gary DeMar continues to argue that the Lord's coming was only in regard to destroying Jerusalem in the first century. For some reason I cannot trick my mind into believing that when the Lord Jesus said to stand up and lift up your heads because your redemption is near he was speaking of destroying the temple then standing as well as Jerusalem.

End Notes

1. Gary DeMar, *War and Rumors of War* [Powder Springs, GA: Americal Vision Press, 2017], ebook, Location 853.

2. John A. Martin, "Luke," in *The Bible Knowledge Commentary; New Testament*, 257.

XVII. Gospel of the Kingdom Preached in the Whole World?

"*And **this gospel of the kingdom will be preached in the whole world** as a testimony to all nations, **and then the end will come**" (Mt. 24:14).

Gary DeMar writes,"*Since the Bible clearly states that that gospel 'was proclaimed in all creation under heaven' (Col.1:23), then the end spoken of by Jesus is a past event for us. Earlier in his letter to the Colossians, Paul describes how the gospel was 'constantly bearing fruit and increasing in all the world [kosmos] (1:6).'*" [1]

DeMar confuses the "gospel of the kingdom" with the "gospel of grace". It was the "gospel of grace" that went to all the world and not the "gospel of the kingdom":

"*The word of the truth of the gospel; Which is come unto you, as it is in all the world; and bringeth forth fruit, as it doth also in you, since the day ye heard of it, and **knew the grace of God in truth**" (Col 1:5,6).

The Apostle Paul was given a ministry to the Jews and one to the Gentiles and in the following verse the Lord speaks about those two ministries:

"*But the Lord said to Ananias, 'Go! This man is my chosen instrument to proclaim my name **to the Gentiles** and their kings and **to the people of Israel**" (Acts 9:15).

In the following passage Paul speaks specifically about those two ministries:

"*But none of these things move me, neither count I my life dear unto myself, so that I might finish my course with joy, and the ministry, which I have received of the Lord Jesus, **to testify the gospel of the grace of God**. And now, behold, I* know that ye all, among whom I have gone **preaching the kingdom of God**, *shall see my face no more*" (Acts 20:24-25; KJV).

The preaching of the "kingdom of God" was the same exact "gospel" which the Twelve preached to the Jews in the following passage:

*"Then he called his twelve disciples together, and gave them power and authority over all devils, and to cure diseases. And he sent them **to preach the kingdom of God**, and to heal the sick...And they departed, and went through the towns, preaching **the gospel**, and healing every where"* (Lk. 9:1-2,6; KJV).

The facts reveal that when they were preaching that gospel the Twelve were not even aware the the Lord Jesus was going to die. After being given that command and after preaching that gospel the transfiguration followed (Lk. 9:29-36; Mk. 9:2-13). Then after the Twelve preached the gospel of the kingdom and after the transfiguration we read the following exchange between the Lord Jesus and the Twelve:

*"They left that place and passed through Galilee. Jesus did not want anyone to know where they were, because he was teaching his disciples. He said to them, 'The Son of Man is going to be delivered into the hands of men. **They will kill him, and after three days he will rise.' But they did not understand what he meant and were afraid to ask him about it**"* (Mk. 9:30-32).

The facts reveal that the Twelve did not even know He was going to die as late as shortly before the Cross:

*"Jesus took the Twelve aside and told them, 'We are going up to Jerusalem, and everything that is written by the prophets about the Son of Man will be fulfilled. He will be delivered over to the Gentiles. They will mock him, insult him and spit on him; they will flog him and **kill him**. On the third day he will rise again.' **The disciples did not understand any of this. Its meaning was hidden from them, and they did not know what he was talking about**"* (Lk. 18:31-34).

104

These facts prove conclusively that the gospel which the Twelve were preaching at Luke 9:6 was not the same gospel which Paul referred to in the following way:

"*For* **the message of the cross,** *is foolishness to those who are perishing,* **but to us who are being saved it is the power of God**" (1 Cor. 1:18.).

The "gospel of the grace of God" cannot be preached apart from the fact that believers are redeemed by the blood of the Lamb (1 Pet. 18-19) and that is exactly the same "redemption" Paul speaks about when declaring the "gospel of the grace of God," that believers "*are justified freely by his grace through* **the redemption that came by Christ Jesus**" (Ro. 3:24).

The Gospel of the Kingdom

Lewis Sperry Chafer. the founding President of Dallas Theological Seminary, said that "*the gospel of the Kingdom...consisted of a legitimate offer to Israel of the promised earthly Davidic kingdom,* **designed particularly for Israel**" [*emphasis added*]. [2]

We will see that the heart and soul of the "gospel of the kingdom" is the truth that Jesus is the Christ, the Son of God. After seeing the spirit descending on the Lord Jesus John the Baptist said,"*and I saw, and bore witness that* **this is the Son of God**" (Jn. 1:34; KJV).

We can know that the Lord Jesus was preaching that He is the Christ by the following conversation between the Lord and some Jews who did not believe in Him:

"*Then came the Jews round about him, and said unto him, How long dost thou make us to doubt?* **If thou be the Christ, tell us plainly. Jesus answered them, I told you, and ye believed not**: *the works that I do in my Father's name, they bear witness of me*" (Jn. 10:24-25; KJV).

After hearing the gospel preached the Ethiopian treasurer asked to be baptized with water: "*And Philip said, If thou believeth with all thine heart, thou mayest. And he answered and said, **I believe that Jesus Christ is the Son of God**"* (Acts 8:37).

The Lord Jesus Himself made it plain that salvation among the Jews depended on their recognizing His "identity":

"*You are from below; I am from above. You are of this world; I am not of this world. **I told you that you would die in your sins; if you do not believe that I am he, you will indeed die in your sins**"* (Jn. 8:23-24).

The following conversation between the Lord Jesus and His disciples concerned His "identity":

"*When Jesus came into the coasts of Caesarea Philippi, he asked his disciples, saying, **Whom do men say that I the Son of man am?** And they said, Some say that thou art John the Baptist: some, Elias; and others, Jeremias, or one of the prophets. He saith unto them, But whom say ye that I am? **And Simon Peter answered and said, Thou art the Christ, the Son of the living God. And Jesus answered and said unto him, Blessed art thou, Simon Barjona**: for flesh and blood hath not revealed it unto thee, but my Father which is in heaven*" (Jn. 16:13-17: KJV).

The Lord Jesus told Peter that he was blessed for believing that Jesus is the Christ, the Son of God, and the following passages tell us how those who believe that truth are blessed:

"***Everyone who believes that Jesus is the Christ is born of God**, and everyone who loves the father loves his child as well. This is how we know that we love the children of God: by loving God and carrying out his commands. In fact, this is love for God: to keep his commands. And his commands are not burdensome, **for everyone born of God overcomes the world. This is the victory that has overcome the world, even our faith. Who is it that overcomes the world? Only the one***

106

who believes that Jesus is the Son of God" (1 Jn. 5:1-5).

"*And many other signs truly did Jesus in the presence of his disciples, which are not written in this book: But these are written, **that ye might believe that Jesus is the Christ, the Son of God; and that believing ye might have life through his name**"* (Jn. 20:30-31; KJV).

Those who believed the truth revealed in the "gospel of the kingdom" were given life when they were born of God:

"*He came to that which was his own, but his own did not receive him. Yet to all who did receive him, **to those who believed in his name, he gave the right to become children of God**--children born not of natural descent, nor of human decision or a husband's will, but **born of God**"* (Jn. 1:11-13).

It is also a simple task to find out what Paul preached to the Jews when he preached the "gospel of the kingdom":

"*Then was Saul certain days with the disciples which were at Damascus. And straightway he preached Christ in **the synagogues**, that he is **the Son of God...proving that this is very Christ.**"* (Acts 9:19-20,22; KJV).

"*Now when they had passed through Amphipolis and Apollonia, they came to Thessalonica, where was a synagogue of the Jews: And Paul, as his manner was, went in unto them, and three sabbath days reasoned with them out of the scriptures, Opening and alleging, that Christ must needs have suffered, and risen again from the dead; and that **this Jesus, whom I preach unto you, is Christ**"* (Acts 17:1-3; KJV).

Romans 1:16

Those who oppose the idea that two different gospels were preached during the Acts period say that the following verse proves that there is only one gospel which saves

"*For I am not ashamed of the gospel, because it is the*

power of God that brings salvation to everyone who believes: first to the Jew, then to the Gentile" (Ro. 1:16).

The Greek word translated "gospel" means "glad tidings" or "good news." The "good news" which was preached first to the Jews was the "gospel of the kingdom" and those who believed that gospel were saved when they believed. The "good news" which was preached to the Gentiles is the "gospel of the grace of God" and all those who believe are saved the moment when they believe it. So there is nothing which Paul wrote in this verse which demands that only one gospel was preached during the Acts period.

Galatians 1:6-9

Other verses that some quote to try to deny the fact that two different gospels were preached during the Acts period are the following words of the Apostle Paul:

*"I am astonished that you are so quickly deserting the one who called you to live in the grace of Christ and are turning to a different gospel--**which is really no gospel at all.** Evidently some people are throwing you into confusion and are trying to pervert the gospel of Christ. But even if we or an angel from heaven should preach a gospel other than the one we preached to you, let them be under God's curse!"* (Gal. 1:6-9).

Here Paul speaks of a "gospel" which perverts the "good news" of Christ and he says that in reality that "gospel" is really no gospel at all. Therefore, he is not telling anyone that if the true "gospel of the kingdom" is preached to them then those preaching that gospel are under God's curse. In fact, after bringing the Gentiles to salvation by the "gospel of the grace of God" Paul did in fact teach them that Jesus is the Christ, the Son of God.

108

End Notes

1. Gary DeMar, *Last Days Madness*, 87.

2. Quoted from G. E. Ladd, *Crucial Questions about the Kingdom of God* (Grand Rapids: Eerdmans, 1952), 50).

Chapter XVIII. The Olive Tree

Let us look at the verses from the eleventh chapter of the epistle to the Romans which speak of the Olive Tree:

*"If the part of the dough offered as firstfruits is holy, then the whole batch is holy; if the root is holy, so are the branches. If some of the branches have been broken off, and you, though a wild olive shoot, have been grafted in among the others and now share in the nourishing sap from the olive root, do not consider yourself to be superior to those other branches. If you do, consider this: You do not support the root, but the root supports you. You will say then, 'Branches were broken off so that I could be grafted in.' Granted. **But they were broken off because of unbelief, and you stand by faith. Do not be arrogant, but tremble. For if God did not spare the natural branches, he will not spare you either**"* (Ro. 11:16-21).

Gary DeMar refers to this passage about the Olive tree and says that the Gentiles have been "grafted in" to the Olive Tree and that the Olive Tree is the Church, the Body of Christ:

*" 'To the Jew first' (Rom. 1:16; 2:9-10), Paul writes, because now, in Christ, 'there is neither Jew nor Greek,' for we 'are all one in Christ Jesus' (Gal. 3:28). **Paul makes the same point in Romans 11 when he describes that the Gentiles were grafted into an existing Jewish body of believers that Acts describes as 'the church' (Rom. 11:12-21)**"* [emphasis added]. [1]

According to Paul some of the Jews were "broken off because of unbelief." How could the Olive Tree be a symbol of the Body of Christ since the Lord Jesus said the following about those who come to Him?:

*"All that the Father giveth me shall come to me; and him that cometh to me **I will in no wise cast out**"* (Jn. 6:37; KJV).

Paul also told the Gentile believers that since *"God did not spare the natural branches, he will not spare you either."* Therefore, if the Olive Tree represents the Body of Christ then no one in the Body enjoys eternal security despite the following words found here:

*"For God so loved the world that he gave his one and only Son, **that whoever believes in him shall not perish but have eternal life**"* (Jn. 3:16).

The "Olive Tree" does not represent the Church, which is His Body. Instead, it represents the "service" of believers. The Olive Tree analogy is in regard to "bearing fruit", or "service". At the time when the nation of Israel was bearing fruit the Lord called them an Olive Tree:

*"The LORD called you a thriving olive tree **with fruit beautiful in form**. But with the roar of a mighty storm he will set it on fire, and its branches will be broken."* (Jer. 11:16).

The Olive Tree was an important tree for the Israelites because it was a source of food and light for them. For hundreds of years the olive was eaten as a staple food and olive oil has been used for cooking and in lamps for light. The oil of the olive was also used for anointing in religious ceremonies.

In regard to bearing fruit the Israelites were appointed to be the LORD's agent upon the earth to bring the gospel to the Gentile nations:

*"For I, the LORD, love justice; I hate robbery and wrongdoing. In my faithfulness I will reward my people and make an everlasting covenant with them. **Their descendants will be known among the nations and their offspring among the peoples**. All who see them will acknowledge that they are a people the LORD has blessed"* (Isa. 61:8-9).

*"Surely you will summon nations you know not, and **nations you do not know will come running to you**, because*

of the LORD your God, the Holy One of Israel, for he has endowed you with splendor" (Isa. 55:5).

Due to the unbelief of many Israelites those people were bearing no fruit for the LORD so they were broken off of the Olive Tree which represents fruit bearing or service. Then when the gospel went to the Gentiles most of those who believed bore fruit for the LORD by serving Him and were therefore grafted into the Olive Tree. But even those believing Gentiles whose service came up short were saved nonetheless:

"*For no one can lay any foundation other than the one already laid, which is Jesus Christ. If anyone builds on this foundation using gold, silver, costly stones, wood, hay or straw, their work will be shown for what it is, because the Day will bring it to light. It will be revealed with fire, and the fire will test the quality of each person's work. If what has been built survives, the builder will receive a reward **If it is burned up, the builder will suffer loss but yet will be saved--** even though only as one escaping through the flames*" (1 Cor. 3:11-15).

End Notes

1. Gary DeMar, *All Promises Made to Israel Have Been Fulfilled: Answering the Replacement Theology Critics* (Part 4); Accessed April 10, 2019, https://americanvision.org/1728/all-promises-made-israel-have-been-fulfilled-answering-replacement-theology-critics-part-4/

Chapter XIX. God Hath Not Cast Away His People

Gary DeMar believes that the theocracy of Israel "went into permanent eclipse" when Jerusalem was destroyed in A.D.70. He says the following and then quotes Harold Fowler:

*"Israel's entire ecclesiastical and political systems were judged when Roman troops sacked, looted, and burned the city...If these cataclysmic events are correctly interpreted as applying to Israel's defeat, then it is clear that immediately after their national disaster of 70 A.D., the once-exalted, unique **theocracy of Israel went into permanent eclipse as God's light-bearers before the nations***" [emphasis added]. [1]

In other words, Gary DeMar holds the belief that the nation of Israel has been forever cast away as God's light-bearer. He writes that *"beyond A.D.70, Israel as a nation plays no prophetic role."* [2]

However, the following promise which the LORD made to the nation of Israel contradicts DeMar's assertion:

*"For the LORD your God is a merciful God; **he will not abandon or destroy you** or forget the covenant with your ancestors, which he confirmed to them by oath"* (Deut. 4:31).

*""For **the LORD will not forsake His people** for His great name's sake: because it hath pleased the LORD to make you His people" (1 Sam. 12:22)."* (1 Sam.2:22; KJV).

In the following passage we can see that it was the physical descendants of Abraham, Isaac and Jacob who made up the nation of Israel whom the Lord chose to be a special people unto Himself:

*"For you are a people holy to the LORD your God. **The**

LORD your God has chosen you out of all the peoples on the face of the earth to be his people, his treasured possession...it was because the LORD loved you and kept the oath he swore to your ancestors that he brought you out with a mighty hand and redeemed you from the land of slavery, from the power of Pharaoh king of Egypt" (Deut. 7:6,8).

The Lord's people in OT times were those of ethnic Israel, the nation according to the flesh, which was redeemed out of Egypt. We can see that same nation described here and we can know that those of the nation were not walking according to the spirit:

"Then the LORD said to Moses, 'Go down, because your people, whom you brought up out of Egypt, have become corrupt. They have been quick to turn away from what I commanded them and have made themselves an idol cast in the shape of a calf. They have bowed down to it and sacrificed to it and have said, 'These are your gods, Israel, who brought you up out of Egypt. '" (Ex. 32:7-8).

So we can see that it was the nation of Israel made up of the physical descendants of Jacob that is spoken of here:

"For the LORD your God is a merciful God; he will not abandon or destroy you or forget the covenant with your ancestors, which he confirmed to them by oath" (Deut. 4:31).

Hath God Cast Away His People?

At the end of the tenth chapter of Romans and the beginning of the eleventh chapter Paul states:

"But to Israel He saith, All day long I have stretched forth my hands unto a disobedient and gainsaying people. I say then, Hath God cast away his people? God forbid" (Ro. 10:21; 11:1; KJV).

In this passage when Paul speaks of Israel it is obvious

that it is Israel which is made up of the physical descendants of Jacob which is in view: "*All day long I have stretched forth my hands unto a disobedient and gainsaying people.*"

Paul is quoting from the OT so his reference to "Israel" at Romans 10:21 must be the Israel which had its beginning in the OT. Here is the verse which he quoted:

"***I have stretched forth my hands all day to a disobedient and gainsaying people***, *to them that walked in a way that was not good, but after their sins. This is the people that provokes me continually in my presence; they offer sacrifices in gardens, and burn incense on bricks to devils, which exist not*" (Isa. 65:2-3; LXX).

So when Paul asks, "Hath God cast away His people" the words "His people" are referring back to the people of whom he just wrote about, the Israel he describes as being "*a disobedient and gainsaying people.*"

Therefore, when Paul asked, "*Hath God cast away His people?*" he was asking if the nation of Israel that had its beginning in the OT had been cast away.

And what he says next makes it plain that God has not cast away the Israel of the OT:

"***God forbid.***"

The Casting Away of Them?

Later in the same chapter Paul speaks of the nation of Israel (them which are my flesh) and says the following:

"*If by any means I may provoke to emulation **them which are my flesh**, and might save some of them. For if **the casting away of them** be the reconciling of the world, what shall the receiving of them be, but life from the dead?*" (Ro. 11:15; KJV).

This translation of Paul's words here directly contradicts

what Paul said earlier, that the Lord *"has not cast away"* national Israel. A better translation is this one:.

*"For if their having been **cast aside** has carried with it the reconciliation of the world, what will their being accepted again be but Life out of death?* (Ro. 11:15; WNT).

The words "cast aside" here are translated from the Greek word *apobole*, and a form of that word (*apoballo*) is translated "throwing...aside" in the following verse:

*"**Throwing his cloak aside**, he jumped to his feet and came to Jesus"* (Mk. 10:50).

A blind man named Bartimaeus was sitting and begging in Jericho when the Lord Jesus entered that city. Bartimaeus cried out, saying, *"Son of David, have mercy on me!"* (v. 48). The crowd told him to stand up because Jesus was calling him. This motivated him to "throw aside" his outer cloak which was spread out before him to collect alms and to rise and to come to the Lord.

Bartimaeus did not "cast away" his garment, but instead he cast it aside in order to facilitate his movement of rising. And the same is true in regard to national Israel. That nation was the LORD's agent to bring the truth of God to the Gentiles but when she denied the Lord Jesus is her promised Messiah the LORD temporarily cast aside her as His agent and He named Paul as the Apostle of the Gentiles (Ro. 11:13).

The Two Divine Programs Are Mutually Exclusive

When the nation of Israel was in covenant relationship with God circumcision was a requirement for the sons of Israel and any uncirumcised male was cut off from that nation:

"This is my covenant, which ye shall keep, between me and you and thy seed after thee; Every man child among you

shall be circumcised. And ye shall circumcise the flesh of your foreskin; and it shall be a token of the covenant betwixt me and you...And the uncircumcised man child whose flesh of his foreskin is not circumcised, that soul shall be cut off from his people; he hath broken my covenant" (Gen. 17:10-11,14).

On the other hand, circumcision profits no one during the Church age, as witnessed by Paul's words here:

"For in Jesus Christ neither circumcision availeth any thing, nor uncircumcision; but faith which worketh by love" (Gal. 5:6).

The Scriptures reveal that when the nation of Israel was in a covenant relationship with the LORD the children of Israel were a special people unto Himself:

"For thou art an holy people unto the LORD thy God: **the LORD thy God hath chosen thee to be a special people unto himself, above all people that are upon the face of the earth"** (Deut.7:6).

On the other hand, during the Church age there are no special people unto the LORD except for believers and in the Body of Christ there is no distinction between the Jews and those of other nationalities:

"And have put on the new man, which is renewed in knowledge after the image of him that created him: **Where there is neither Greek nor Jew, circumcision nor uncircumcision,** *Barbarian, Scythian, bond nor free: but Christ is all, and in all"* (Col. 3:10-11).

Norman L. Geisler writes the following about Colossians 3:10-11:

*"In Christ distinctions are removed. These include national distinctions (**Greek or Jew**...); religious distinctions (**circumcised or uncircumcised**)..."* [3]

These facts serve to prove that when the LORD's program for Israel is in view then that program cannot be about the Body of Christ because His two different programs are mutually exclusive. In other words, when the Divine plan toward Israel is in effect then the children of Israel are above all people on the face of the earth so therefore it is impossible that at the same time the Divine plan is also toward the Body of Christ where there is no difference between the Jews and the Gentiles. Sir Robert Anderson wrote the following:

"For just as we aver that 'God cannot lie,' we may assert that He cannot act at the same time upon two wholly different and incompatible principles." [4]

When the LORD is dealing with the Body of Christ His program toward Israel is in abeyance. Also, a sharp divide is seen at the end of the church age when the saints will be caught up to meet the Lord Jesus in the air. Once that happens the Body of Christ will be removed from the earth and that will pave the way for Israel to be restored to her previous position as a people above all people on the face of the earth.

End Notes

1. Gary DeMar, *Last Days Madness*, 152-153.

2. *Ibid.*, 398.

3. Norman L. Geisler, "Colossians," in *The Bible Knowledge Commentary; New Testament*, 681.

4. Sir Robert Anderson, *Forgotten Truths* (Grand Rapids: Kregel Publications, 1980), 44.

Chapter XX. Conclusion

A Challenge

Gary DeMar writes that *"I want to be challenged by the best arguments possible, whether they come from full preterists or dispensationalists."* [1]

Being a dispensationalist I challenge Gary DeMar's theology on many different fronts. First, I challenge his assertion concerning what will happen at the "end of the age." He says that the end of the age has already come and gone but the Lord Jesus spoke of a world wide harvest happening then. I challenge Dr. DeMar to answer why anyone should believe that when the Lord says that the "field" that will be harvested at the "end of the age" is the "world (*kosmos*)" that He really meant that the field is only Judea and Jerusalem.

Also, perhaps Gary DeMar will answer why the Lord Jesus would speak of a judgment coming upon the "inhabited earth (*oikoumene*)" after the great tribulation comes to an end if that prophecy was fulfilled in A.D.70 in Jerusalem and Judea--especially since he said the following:

"When first-century Christians read the word 'oikoumene,' they thought of what they knew of their world" [*emphasis mine*]. [2]

Also, I challenge Gary DeMar to defend his teaching that all the land promises which the LORD made to Israel have already been fulfilled despite the following promise the LORD made to David about the land:

"Now therefore so shalt thou say unto my servant David...I will appoint a place for my people Israel, and will

*plant them, that they may dwell in a place of their own, **and move no more; neither shall the children of wickedness afflict them any more, as beforetime*** (2 Sam. 7:8,10; KJV).

A Spirit of Grace

Next, I challenge Gary DeMar to explain why anyone should believe that the following passage refers to the destruction of Jerusalem in A.D. 70 since the passage speaks of the LORD pouring out a Spirit of grace on the inhabitants of Jerusalem:

*"On that day I will set out to destroy all the nations that attack Jerusalem. And **I will pour out on the house of David and the inhabitants of Jerusalem a spirit of grace** and supplication...On that day **a fountain will be opened** to the house of David and the inhabitants of Jerusalem, **to cleanse them from sin and impurity**"* (Zech. 12:8-10, 13:1).

In regard to this passage DeMar writes:

*"More than a million Jews died at the hands of the Roman army. Their Savior had come, and they had crucified Him forty years earlier. **Again the language of judgment is familiar to students of the Old Testament: 'And I will pour out on the house of David and on the inhabitants of Jerusalem, the Spirit of grace and supplication**, so that they will look upon Me whom they have pierced; and they will mourn for Him, as one mourns for an only son, and they will weep bitterly over Him, like the bitter weeping over a first-born' (Zech. 12:10)" [emphasis mine].* [3]

Despite the fact that the passage from the book of Zechariah speaks of the LORD destroying the nations that attack Jerusalem and His pouring out upon that city a Spirit of grace and cleansing the Jews of their sins De Mar asserts that event occured in A.D. 70 so he thinks that the following prophecy of the Lord Jesus is describing the fulfillment of Zechariah 12:8-10:

*"For this is **the time of punishment** in fulfillment of all that has been written. How dreadful it will be in those days for pregnant women and nursing mothers! There will be great distress in the land and **wrath against this people. They will fall by the sword and will be taken as prisoners to all the nations**"* (Lk. 21:22-24).

Those events certainly are not describing the LORD destroying all the nations which come against Jerusalem nor do they speak of Him pouring out a Spirit of grace among the Jews or of cleansing them from their sins. The following passage describes a time in the future when the passage from the book of Zechariah will be fulfilled:

*"For I will take you out of the nations; I will gather you from all the countries and bring you back into your own land. **I will sprinkle clean water on you, and you will be clean**; I will cleanse you from all your impurities and from all your idols. I will give you a new heart and **put a new spirit in you**; I will remove from you your heart of stone and give you a heart of flesh"* (Ez. 36:24-26).

Zechariah 14

Let us now take a look at the following verses and examine Gary DeMar's interpretation of them:

2 *"I will gather all the nations to Jerusalem to fight against it; the city will be captured, the houses ransacked, and the women raped. Half of the city will go into exile, but the rest of the people will not be taken from the city."*

3 *"Then the LORD will go out and fight against those nations, as he fights on a day of battle."*

4 *"On that day his feet will stand on the Mount of Olives, east of Jerusalem"* (Zech. 14:2-4).

In regard to verse two, Gary DeMar says: *"This happened when the Roman armies, made up of soldiers from the nations it conquered, went to war against Jerusalem...Zechariah is describing the events surrounding Jerusalem's destruction in A.D.70." [4]*

He then attempts to explain verse three, saying, *"After using Rome as His rod to smite Jerusalem, God turns on Rome in judgment." [5]*

Since the Lord did not fight against the nation of Rome during the destruction of Jerusalem in A.D.70 Gary DeMar quotes G.N.M Collins: *"It is significant **that the decline of the Roman Empire** dates from the fall of Jerusalem"* [emphasis mine]. [6]

Gary DeMar continues: *"Thomas Scott concurs: 'It is also observable, that the Romans after having been made the executioners of divine vengence on the Jewish nation, **never prospered as they had done before**; but the Lord evidently fought against them, and all the nations which composed their overgrown empire; till at last it was subverted, and their fairest cities and provinces were ravaged by barbarous invaders' "*[emphasis mine]. [7]

According to Gary DeMar the battle when the Lord fights against the nations that came against Jerusalem is nothing more than the idea that the Roman Empire "never prospered as they had before." We are supposed to believe that this battle was not really a battle but instead only represents the beginning of the decline of the Roman Empire where she "never prospered as they had done before".

However, Zechariah wrote, *"Then the LORD will go out and fight against those nations, as he fights on a day of battle."* (Zech. 14:3).

"As He fights in the day of battle"! These words should lead those who read them to think of the following events which describe the Lord as a "Warrior."

"The LORD is a warrior; the LORD is his name. Pharaoh's chariots and his army he has hurled into the sea. The best of Pharaoh's officers are drowned in the Red Sea"

(Ex. 15:3-4).

If the Lord is going to fight against those nations *"as He fights in the day of battle"* then the battle will not be a matter of a single nation *"not prospering"* as she did before but instead it will be comparable to when the Lord destroyed Pharaoh's army.

The battle which Zechariah describes is not in regard to a decline of a single nation that lasts for hundreds years until at last she is subverted! Instead, it will happen in the same day when the LORD will pour out the Spirit of grace upon Jerusalem:

"On that day I will set out to destroy all the nations that attack Jerusalem. *And I will pour out on the house of David and the inhabitants of Jerusalem a spirit of grace and supplication"* (Zech. 12:8).

Gary DeMar employs what Robert L. Thomas describes as an "extreme allegorical approach" of interpreting prophecy. This approach leaves his interpretations lacking any resemblance to what Zechariah originally wrote. He does not seem to realize that his method of interpreting these verses brings prophecy into contempt and ridicule.

Gary DeMar has been deceived into believing that these prophecies have already been fulfilled and now he is unwittingly deceiving others. He continues to turn his ears from the truth and in doing so he is now misleading others into believing teachings which are nothing more than fables.

Sir Robert Anderson writes:*"In no other sphere save that of religion do men of intelligence and culture willingly subject their minds to delusions. The historic Church once tried to compel belief that this planet was the fixed centre of the solar system; but who believes it now? Men cannot be made to believe that water runs uphill, or that five and five make anything but ten. In no other sphere can they be induced to stultify reason and common sense. But in religion there seems to be no limit to their credulity."* [8]

The teaching concerning the Last Days promoted by Gary DeMar and the rest of the Preterists is easily shown to be nothing more than delusions.

The Man of Lawlessness

We have been looking at the Preterists' distorted teaching about the day of the LORD (Zech. 14:1-4) now let us look at Paul's words in regard to that day as it pertains to the "man of lawlessness":

*"Don't let anyone deceive you in any way, for that day (the day of the LORD) will not come until the rebellion occurs and **the man of lawlessness is revealed**, the man doomed to destruction. He will oppose and will exalt himself over everything that is called God or is worshiped, **so that he sets himself up in God's temple, proclaiming himself to be God**"* (2 Thess. 2:3-4).

When I first became aware of this passage my first thought was how will it be possible for the man of lawlessness to deceive others to such an extent that he can actually have access to God's temple and declare himself to be God since the Bible warns about such a man. However, when I became aware of Preterism which teaches that the man of lawlessness belongs to past history I had my answer. According to Gary DeMar there is no reason to be on guard for the appearance of the man of lawlessness because he has already come and gone:

*"**New Testament preterism relates to prophecies that were fulfilled in events leading up to and including the destruction of the temple and the judgment on the city of Jerusalem that took place in A.D. 70, in particular**, the Olivet Discourse in the Synoptic Gospels (Matt. 24; Mark 13; Luke 21), **the Man of Lawlessness (2 Thess. 2)**, passages related to the Antichrist (1 John 2:18, 22; 4:3; 2 John 7), and, of course, Revelation (1:1, 3; 22:10)"* [emphasis

added].[9]

End Notes

1. Gary DeMar, "Is Gary DeMar Secretly a Friend to Hyperpreterists?" *The American Vision*; Accessed December 27, 2018, https://americanvision.org/3032/is-gary-demar-secretly-a-friend-to-hyperpreterists/

2. Gary DeMar, *The Gospel Preached to All the World*, Part 3 of 4; Accessed November 22, 2018, https://www.preteristarchive.com/Modern/2003_demar_all-the-world.html

3. Gary DeMar, *Last Days Madness*, 167.

4. *Ibid.*, 438.

5. *Ibid.*, 439.

6. *Ibid.*

7. *Ibid.*

8. Sir Robert Anderson, *The Bible or the Church?* (London: Pickering & Inglis, Second Edition), 61.

9. Gary DeMar, "Is Gary DeMar Secretly a Friend to Hyperpreterists?" *The American Vision*; Accessed December 27, 2018, https://americanvision.org/3032/is-gary-demar-secretly-a-friend-to-hyperpreterists/

The author encourages edifying discussion regarding this book. Please contact him via email at jerryshugart2@yahoo.com

MORE BIBLICAL INSTRUCTION FROM GERALD B. SHUGART

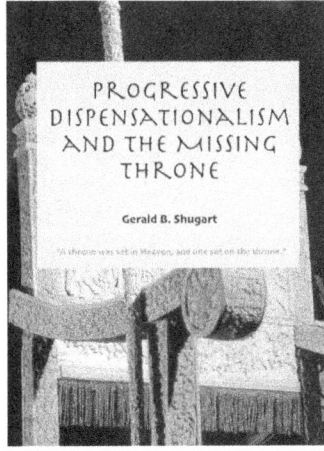

Progressive Dispensationalism and the Missing Throne

A well-guided Spiritual expedition into one of the most confusing aspects of modern theology today.

Do those in the Body of Christ partake of the New Covenant promised to the nation of Israel at Jeremiah 31:31-34? The failure of the Traditional Dispensationalists to adequately answer that question has led to Progressive Dispensationalism, a system of Bible study that undermines the very foundation upon which Traditional Dispensationalism has been built. This book proves beyond any doubt that those in the Body of Christ do not receive spiritual blessings through that covenant but instead those blessings are received through the gospel of Christ. Sir Robert Anderson wrote that "our spiritual and eternal blessings do not depend on a covenant made with us, but upon a testament under which we are beneficiaries." Exceptional and exciting Biblical truths for Christians abound in this valuable and intellectually incisive volume, a book that addresses a theological mystery.

ALSO AVAILABLE FROM GERALD B. SHUGART

SIR ROBERT ANDERSON - The Thinking Man's Guide to the Bible

Biblical insight by the real life Sherlock Holmes who solved the "Jack the Ripper" case.

Sir Robert Anderson, KCB (29 May 1841 – 15 November 1918), was the Chief of the Criminal Investigation Departament of Scotland Yard from 1888 to 1901. He was also an intelligence officer, theologian and writer.

Author Gerald B. Shugart presents an intriguing historical panorama of the Biblical studies and spiritual insight of Sir Robert Anderson, the individual responsible for the investigation of the man known the world over as "Jack the Ripper" in Victorian-era London. Fully referenced.

Gerald Shugart's books are available in both Kindle and print format. Print copies are available wherever books are sold.

www.ingramcontent.com/pod-product-compliance
Lightning Source LLC
Chambersburg PA
CBHW032103080426
42733CB00006B/394